Montgomery

The World Generals Series

"Palgrave's World Generals Series will feature great leaders whose reputations have transcended their own nations, whose bold characters led to new forms of combat, whose determination and courage gave shape to new dynasties and civilizations—men whose creativity and courage inspired multitudes. Beginning with illustrious World War II German Field Marshal Irwin Rommel, known as the Desert Fox, the series will shed new light on famous warrior-leaders like Napoleon, Frederick the Great, Alexander, Julius Caesar, Genghis Khan, drawing out the many important leadership lessons that are still relevant to our lives today."

—General Wesley K. Clark (Ret.)

This distinguished new series will feature the lives of eminent military leaders from around the world who changed history. Top military historians will write concise but comprehensive biographies including the personal lives, battles, strategies and legacies of these great generals, with the aim to provide background and insight into contemporary armies and wars as well as to draw lessons for the leaders of today.

Rommel by Charles Messenger

Alexander the Great by Bill Yenne

Montgomery by Trevor Royle

Lafayette by Marc Leepson

Ataturk by Austin Bay

De Gaulle by Michael Haskew

Giap by James Warren

Julius Caesar by Bill Yenne

Montgomery

Lessons in Leadership from the Soldier's General

Trevor Royle

palgrave
macmillan

First published in 2010 by
PALGRAVE MACMILLAN®
in the US—a division of St. Martin's Press LLC,
175 Fifth Avenue, New York, NY 10010.

Where this book is distributed in the UK, Europe and the rest of the world,
this is by Palgrave Macmillan, a division of Macmillan Publishers Limited,
registered in England, company number 785998, of Houndmills,
Basingstoke, Hampshire RG21 6XS.

Palgrave Macmillan is the global academic imprint of the above companies
and has companies and representatives throughout the world.

Palgrave® and Macmillan® are registered trademarks in the United States,
the United Kingdom, Europe and other countries.

ISBN: 978–0–230–61489–5

Library of Congress Cataloging-in-Publication Data

Royle, Trevor.
    Montgomery : lessons in leadership from the soldier's general / Trevor
Royle.
      p. cm.
    Includes bibliographical references and index.
    ISBN 978–0–230–61489–5 (hardback)
     1. Montgomery of Alamein, Bernard Law Montgomery, Viscount,
1887–1976—Military leadership. 2. World War,
1939–1945—Campaigns. 3. Generals—Great Britain—Biography.
4. Great Britain. Army—Biography. 5. World War, 1939–1945—
Biography. 6. Command of troops—Case studies. I. Title.

DA69.3.M56R69 2010
940.54′1241092—dc22   2010012674

A catalogue record of the book is available from the British Library.

Design by Newgen Imaging Systems (P) Ltd., Chennai, India.

First PALGRAVE MACMILLAN paperback edition: December 2010

10 9 8 7 6 5 4 3 2 1

Printed in the United States of America.

Contents

Illustrations appear between pages 116 and 117.

Foreword

MUCH CRITICIZED AND MUCH REVERED, BRITISH FIELD MARSHAL Bernard Montgomery epitomized much of the best and worst of alliance warfare in the twentieth century. Insightful, self-righteous, and arrogant, Montgomery won some battles brilliantly but created infuriating conflict and distrust among his peers. Both the winning and the feuding are worthy of serious reflection.

Trevor Royle's excellent, fast-paced biography of Montgomery draws out all the lessons and sets them skillfully in their strategic context. Especially for contemporary readers, this is particularly useful. Montgomery, after all, was an officer of the British Empire, and his story is also the story of the sad and inevitable replacement of this nineteenth century empire by the upstart American "empire" of the twentieth century. Probably no single leader lived this transition more personally and painfully than Montgomery.

"Monty," as he was known, was born in a church family, raised principally by a firm mother whose strong convictions played no small role in forming the fierce character he later displayed on so many occasions. He was scrappy and determined as a youngster and early on committed to make the army his career. His Sandhurst record showed his keen leadership abilities; upon graduation he became an infantry officer.

It is here that his experiences began to diverge so greatly from those of his future allies. Montgomery saw the British Army in India, with its sense of entitlement and laxity, and he saw the failures of the early British actions against the Germans in World War I. Wounded in early fighting, he recovered and returned to the theater to serve on divisional and corps staff, where he developed expertise in training, organizational discipline, and high-level staff leadership. None of his American contemporaries had seen so much of the First World War's often senseless slaughter and frustrations or were any more determined to remedy it through their own efforts.

The interwar years found Monty, like his American contemporaries, reduced in rank, sent to various schools for military studies, and serving at home and abroad. In Montgomery's case it was the Middle East—Palestine and Egypt. In the late 1930's, as a British two-star general, he would have outranked his future colleagues Eisenhower, Patton, and Bradley. And by late 1939, while the American Army was struggling to mobilize and modernize, and Ike was leaving command of a battalion, Monty was commanding the British Third Infantry Division in Belgium—his second divisional command—and preparing to defend against a German onslaught. No wonder he carried a certain "attitude" into his later work with the Americans.

When the German blitzkrieg came, Montgomery's force was part of a general British withdrawal that ended up in the evacuation at Dunkirk. But his outfit performed brilliantly, thanks to his concepts of "grip"—thinking through alternatives, training, rehearsals, morale-building around the plans, and controlled execution—and the "directed telescope"—junior officers from his headquarters liaising directly with his frontline units and bringing back current, eyewitness battlefield knowledge. It was his success here, and his dedication to these principles in future battles, that were responsible for his rise to the highest levels of command. And it was precisely when these approaches were compromised in higher-level operational command that he found himself in the most trouble.

Pushed into high command of the British Eighth Army in 1942 in North Africa, he followed two more senior and rather more "respectable" predecessors who had met misfortune at Rommel's hand. Montgomery's fighting spirit, stubborn insistence on overwhelming material superiority, and trademark "grip" on the ensuing battle brought Britain and the Allies their greatest victory yet over the Germans and Rommel at the battle of El Alamein in November 1942.

But from there onward, Montgomery, like Great Britain herself, had to contend with the rising power of the United States. Monty was competitive and supremely confident. He was a battle-proven winner. He stood firm on his ideas, often to a fault. In his clashes with Eisenhower and the American General's Lieutenants Patton and Bradley, he was in some way simply representing Britain's gradual and somewhat resentful surrender of Alliance leadership. As Monty seemed to learn the hard way, Alliance leadership goes to those who field the greatest forces and shoulder the greatest burdens. And by early 1943 the British forces were far outmatched by the American contributions.

Monty fought to get his way in the subsequent invasion of Sicily and succeeded, even though Patton's audacious style showed him up in execution. Soon thereafter he fought for his approach in the cross-Channel invasion of France at Normandy. Again, he got his plan adopted, but Ike refused him the title of Land Force Commander. And in the execution of the breakout, British forces failed to meet his own ambitious timetable, partly due to his own failure to adequately understand the Normandy battlefield around Caen and apply fully his own training principles. In the autumn of 1944, Monty got his way again, with the Market-Garden thrust toward the lower Rhine, only to fail due to faulty intelligence and flawed execution. He recovered his reputation reprising Bradley's failures in the December 1944 Battle of the Bulge and then led the northern Allied thrust into Germany.

But the fights with Eisenhower and his team, and even the British flag officers on Ike's team, took their toll on his reputation and impacted Monty's own outlook. He was a contentious and believed-by-many vainglorious figure. He had no friends among the American camp.

When I arrived at Supreme Headquarters, Allied Powers, Europe, in the late 1970s as a Major on General Alexander Haig's staff, I learned of him by his reputation there. He had become the first NATO Deputy Supreme Allied Commander, Europe, a post which he held for many years and in which he exercised considerable influence in NATO's early years. Two decades after he left active service, Montgomery's reputation lingered in NATO—in the outlook, in the training regimen, and in the veneration in which he was held by his British Army subordinates. I studied him assiduously and used his training approach in numerous assignments in the U.S. Army as we were recovering from Vietnam. We embedded his concept of "grip" in our training centers at battalion, brigade, and division levels and worked hard to develop the foresight and organizational discipline that Montgomery achieved in his finest units.

But there's no excusing the rancor he created. Montgomery quarreled, plotted, and sniped. He questioned competence and motive. And he made himself difficult. No doubt it hurt professionally to see obviously less experienced Americans coming into higher command positions. But others managed the transition with considerably more grace.

In Alliance warfare, commanders must endeavor to work in greatest harmony and build ever-deeper trust. It isn't always easy, as I learned for myself in NATO command in the late 1990s. But, at most levels of warfare, and in almost every situation, there's more than one way to solve a problem. Allied cohesion at higher levels is often more important than a specific tactical or operational solution. And so, commanders must increasingly strive for the right balance between their own determination of what will work militarily and the larger teamwork that their efforts comprise.

Trevor Royle's biography lays this all out, with the clarity of over sixty years' perspective on the key events. It's a gripping read, worthy of serious attention.

—General Wesley K. Clark (ret.)

British and U.S. Army Ranks

British Army	U.S. Army
Field Marshal (no longer used)	General of the Army
General	General
Lieutenant-General	Lieutenant General
Major-General	Major General
Brigadier	Brigadier General
Colonel	Colonel
Lieutenant-Colonel	Lieutenant Colonel
Major	Major
Captain	Captain
Lieutenant	First Lieutenant
Second Lieutenant	Second Lieutenant
—	Chief Warrant Officer
Warrant Officer First Class	Warrant Officer
Warrant Officer Second Class	—
Staff Sergeant	Sergeant Major
Sergeant	Master Sergeant
—	First Sergeant
—	Sergeant First Class
—	Staff Sergeant

British Army	U.S. Army
—	Sergeant
Corporal	Corporal
Lance-Corporal	Private First Class
Private	Private

Structure of British Army 1939–1945

Army Group (11th, 15th, 18th, 21st)
Army (First, Second, Eighth, Ninth, Tenth, Twelfth, Fourteenth)
Corps (I–XIII, XXV, XXX)
Division: Armoured and Infantry
Independent Infantry Brigades and Brigade Groups
Brigade: Armoured and Infantry
Commandos and Special Forces
Regiment: Armoured, Artillery, Engineers, Signals
Battalion, Infantry (the operational element of an Infantry Regiment)

British Abbreviations
Used in the Text

ACIGS	Assistant Chief of the Imperial General Staff
AG	Adjutant-General
AVM	Air Vice-Marshal
BAOR	British Army of the Rhine
BEF	British Expeditionary Force
BGS	Brigadier, General Staff
CDS	Chief of the Defence Staff
CIGS	Chief of the Imperial General Staff
COS	Chief of Staff
COSSAC	Chief of Staff to the Supreme Allied Commander
DMI	Director of Military Intelligence
DMO	Director of Military Operations
DSO	Distinguished Service Order
GCB	Knight, Grand Cross of the Bath
GOC	General Officer Commanding
LO	Liaison Officer
MA	Military Assistant
MC	Military Cross

MP	Member of Parliament
NA	National Archives (Kew, London)
NATO	North Atlantic Treaty Organization
OBE	Order of the British Empire
PRO	Public Record Office
RAF	Royal Air Force
RN	Royal Navy
SHAEF	Supreme Headquarters Allied Expeditionary Force
SHAPE	Supreme Headquarters Allied Powers in Europe
TA	Territorial Army
VC	Victoria Cross
VCIGS	Vice Chief of the Imperial General Staff
WO	War Office
WU	Western Union

Introduction

THE BRITISH FIELD MARSHAL WAS NOT AMUSED. WEARING BATTLE DRESS and his trademark black beret with two badges—one of the Royal Tank Regiment, the other of a field marshal—he stood framed in the door of his campaign caravan and testily regarded the four visitors standing outside. "Who are you?" he asked, with a tone that suggested he had just encountered an unpleasant smell. Beneath the British national flag that had been specially raised for this purpose in a copse of silver birches on the rolling expanse of Lüneberg Heath in northern Germany, four smartly dressed German officers snapped to attention. On the right end of the line, the first, wearing a black leather greatcoat, replied tersely, "General Admiral von Friedeburg, commander in chief of the German navy, sir."

In an equally peremptory fashion, the sprightly field marshal shot back, "I have never heard of you."

It was the morning of May 3, 1945, and Bernard Law Montgomery was in his element. In front of him stood four German plenipotentiaries representing Grand Admiral Karl von Dönitz, the recently appointed *Reichsführer* (leader of Germany), following the suicide of Adolf Hitler a few days earlier. As the other officers announced themselves, Montgomery looked icily at each one in turn.

The last and most junior was tall and dressed in the uniform of a Gestapo officer. He announced himself as Major Friedl.

"Major!" snapped Montgomery. "How dare you bring a major into my Headquarters!"[1]

The humiliation was complete; the commander of the British 21st Army Group was intent on humbling his defeated opponents, proffering a casual right hand to his beret in reply to their smart salutes. He had come a long way to reach this moment—from the defeat of the British Army at Dunkirk in 1940 through the first victories in North Africa and in Sicily in 1942–1943 to the long crusade that had taken the Allies from Normandy to the Elbe River—and he was determined to savor it.

But there was more to Montgomery's performance than an exercise in mortification. He knew that the German officers had come to surrender, and he also understood that they wanted to get the best terms possible, by posing as undefeated opponents.

"What do you want?" he barked at von Friedeburg. The response was staggering: the Germans were asking to surrender not the forces facing the Allies to the north but three German armies fighting the Soviet Red Army to the east, between Rostock and Berlin. Montgomery was having none of it. He curtly told them to approach the Soviet high command instead, and countered with his own proposal that the Germans should surrender unconditionally all their forces in northern Germany, the Netherlands, and Denmark. It was not an idle request, as the war correspondent of *Time* magazine recorded: "With the ultimate gesture of military scorn, he took them into his tent and showed them where they stood—on his own battle operations map. Then he sent them off to lunch."[2]

Later that afternoon, suitably nourished but red-eyed with strain and exhaustion, von Friedeburg agreed to return to the German high command headquarters at Flensburg to obtain formal permission to accept Montgomery's offer. That evening the victorious field marshal sent a telegram to Field Marshal Sir Alan Brooke, the British Chief of the Imperial General Staff (CIGS), giving him the good news: "I think they will agree to surrender unconditionally all forces as they are now quite clear as to the hopelessness of their situation."[3]

The German response arrived the next day when von Friedeburg returned late in the afternoon to sign the surrender document at Montgomery's tactical headquarters outside the village of Wendisch. Once again, as Montgomery recorded in his memoirs, the German officers were reminded that they were on the losing side with an absence of pomp and circumstance: "The arrangements in the tent were very simple—a trestle table covered with an army blanket, an inkpot, an ordinary army pen that you could buy in a store for two pence. There were two BBC [British Broadcasting Corporation] microphones on the table."[4]

The Germans signed the instrument of surrender first, followed by Montgomery, who did so "on behalf of the Supreme Allied Commander General Eisenhower," dating the document to the left of the German signatures, together with his name and rank, B. L. Montgomery, Field Marshal. It was 6:30 P.M. on May 4, 1945.

This was the pinnacle of Montgomery's career. Few army commanders ever get the opportunity to receive the surrender in the field of a defeated enemy, and he certainly made the most of the opportunity, sensing the drama of the moment and the role that he had played in it. After almost six years of conflict, the war in Europe had finally come to an end, and a vicious enemy had been defeated; as a result, on that spring evening on the expanse of Lüneberg Heath, Montgomery was master of all he surveyed.

That moment was also the zenith of his power. By any standards he was the greatest British army commander of the Second World War and one of the most successful generals in the Allied coalition. Thanks to his showmanship, he was also one of the best known, though not always for the right reasons: his divisive and fractious nature was disliked by his senior colleagues, who found him conceited and overbearing.

Those well-known personal shortcomings have invariably colored assessments of him as a soldier throughout the years, but Montgomery was never less than an inspirational commander and a dedicated battlefield tactician. He was a meticulous planner, created maximum support, had an ability to grasp the essentials of any military problem, insisted on thorough training, and, above all, had a determination to beat the enemy with minimum casualties in his own forces. In North Africa in 1942, he took over command of the demoralized British Eighth Army and quickly turned around its fortunes by displaying energy and commitment and instilling the will to win. In the pursuit phase into Tunisia and during the campaign in Sicily, Montgomery demonstrated a less adept touch. Not always able to exploit a fluid situation, his caution often became a burden, but during the planning for the invasion of Sicily, he proved himself to be a splendid organizer and a great believer in the effectiveness of simple tactics. Those virtues came to his aid during the planning for Operation Overlord in June 1944. It was due to his influence that the weight of the Allied attack was increased, and the success of D-Day owes much to his farsightedness.

Of course, like any battlefield commander, Montgomery had his faults. During the advance into northwest Europe, he failed to move his forces beyond the port of Antwerp to cut off retreating German forces, and he was responsible for the failure of the airborne attack at Arnhem (Operation Market-Garden). He also failed to grasp the dynamics of coalition warfare and was not what might be called a team player. After U.S. General Dwight D. Eisenhower assumed overall command of Allied operations in September 1944, the relationship between the two men soured, and on several occasions Montgomery was fortunate to keep his job. Among other foolish comments, he enraged U.S. Generals Omar N. Bradley and George S. Patton by claiming responsibility for winning the Battle of the Bulge in the winter of 1944–1945. His overweening behavior infuriated his U.S. allies and frequently threatened unity within the alliance.

Among his own soldiers, though, the men who owed him their lives, he was given nothing but adulation and—uncommonly for a general—he was able to transcend the relationship between the leader and the led. Montgomery was at his best on the battlefield, especially before engagement, when meticulous planning was essential. An inspirational commander whose self-confidence was legendary, Montgomery's career was directed by the simple credo that the profession of arms was a lifelong study, and he devoted himself to it with the passion and intensity of a committed Christian. That motto informed everything he accomplished as a soldier and underpinned the values that he brought to the command of great armies in an age of total war.

CHAPTER ONE

An Uncertain Education

BERNARD LAW MONTGOMERY WAS BORN ON NOVEMBER 17, 1887, IN Kennington, South London, the third son and fourth child of the Reverend Henry Hutchinson Montgomery and his wife, Maud Farrar. Both families were distinguished. On his father's side, the Montgomerys were landowners; solidly Protestant and Anglo-Irish, they were descended from the steady stream of English settlers who had moved to Ireland in the centuries after the Norman settlement of 1169. With their New Park estate at Moville, near Londonderry, in Northern Ireland, the Montgomerys were well established—the nearest British equivalent to the equally aristocratic landowning Prussian Junker class. And, just as the Junkers produced soldiers for the Prussian and German armies, so too did many nineteenth- and twentieth-century British generals come from Anglo-Irish origins. The Duke of Wellington was the son of an Irish peer, and, later in the century, Field

Marshals Garnet Wolseley, Frederick Roberts, and Horatio Herbert Kitchener all enjoyed close links with Ireland. In Montgomery's own generation, fellow Field Marshals Harold Alexander and Alan Brooke were born into families with backgrounds in Northern Ireland.

Bernard's grandfather Sir Robert Montgomery did not serve as a soldier but he belonged to an equally exalted class, working as an imperial administrator with the Indian Civil Service, the so-called "heaven-born" who directed British rule in India. In time he became lieutenant governor of Punjab, one of the largest Indian states. His second son, Henry, the future field marshal's father, was educated at Harrow School and Trinity College, Cambridge, and entered the Church of England to emerge as an ambitious, progressive, and energetic cleric. In 1887 he was the priest at St. Mary's Church, where he enjoyed the friendship and patronage of Canon Frederick William Farrar, the rector of St. Margaret's, the Westminster church traditionally associated with the House of Commons. Farrar was one of the better-known men of his day. He was not only a liberal reformer with a wide circle of literary and political friends, he was also the author of *Eric, or Little by Little* (1858), a sentimental and melodramatic novel set in an English private school that enjoyed a huge readership in its day. (Today it is little more than a literary curiosity.) Through the association with Farrar, the young curate was introduced to his family and became engaged to Maud, their third daughter, when she was only 14. Two years later, they married.

Both parents and the lives they led would have a profound effect on Bernard's upbringing. His father was reserved, single-minded, and hardworking and left the rearing of children to his wife. However, Maud Montgomery was by any standards a troubled woman. Not only was she very young, little more than a child herself, she found marriage to be a lonely and unsettling experience. Her husband was 18 years her senior, an ambitious and conscientious cleric with a busy parish of 14,000, and he concentrated on his work rather than his wife. Maud later admitted that she was often lonely and could remember "sitting in the drawing room and crying bitterly" when she was left alone in the house.[1] Her only role was motherhood: a family was started immediately, and she eventually gave birth to three daughters and six sons.

In 1889, Montgomery senior was appointed Bishop of Tasmania, and the family traveled by steamship to Hobart, the capital of the colony, where they took up residence in the bishop's house overlooking the estuary on the Derwent River. From the outset of his appointment, Bishop Montgomery approached his work with missionary zeal. "A man must be a leader in the Colonies," he described his role. "The quiet harmless man will fail. It is all push."[2] In addition to overseeing the completion of the new cathedral in Hobart, the bishop spent months at a time traveling to remote areas, including the west coast mining settlements and the Bass Strait region. He also visited New Guinea and Melanesia and envisaged the creation of an Anglican church in Australia that would embrace dioceses in the Pacific region. "It is because the work is all Missionary here that I love it so," he told Frederick Temple, archbishop of Canterbury, in 1901. "Great questions such as Education, Temperance, Social problems between classes, come to me as *duties*. Missionary questions come to me as *joys*."[3] In that role, Bishop Montgomery believed that the church had to set high moral standards and bear witness to an uncorrupted life.

Laudable though those efforts were, they came at a cost to family harmony. While her husband was away, Maud was left to fend for herself and bring up her family alone. Money was often scarce, and the bishop took delight in the local assertion that his wife was considered the worst-dressed woman in Hobart. Left to her own devices, Maud instituted military-style discipline in the home. Her standards were not only strict but brooked no disagreement with her methods. One biographer states that in her case, "Rule was all. Sin had to be closely watched,"[4] and there is evidence to suggest that she could be tyrannical with her children. In his memoirs, Montgomery wrote that he experienced "an absence of affectionate understanding of the problems facing the young, certainly as far as the five elder children were concerned."[5] He also claimed that he was in a constant state of confrontation with his mother, engaged in a battle of wills, which she inevitably won. These altercations were accompanied by regular canings, and Montgomery was not afraid to admit that as a boy he behaved badly. Education was left in the hands of tutors imported from England, and the schooling was run on strict disciplinary lines.

Later in life, Montgomery would take a great deal of interest in the childhoods of other great military commanders and claimed that a strict or harsh upbringing had been a determining factor in their careers. It is possible that he was attempting to find a common denominator that would link him to other great captains—he identified the Dukes of Wellington (rightly) and Marlborough (wrongly) as having endured lonely and harsh childhoods—but there is other evidence from British military history to support his contention. Field Marshal Lord Kitchener was regularly punished by his father by being spread-eagled with his ankles and wrists tied to tent pegs, and the memoirs of Victorian soldiers like T. E. Lawrence (Lawrence of Arabia) contain accounts of strict upbringings that may sound cruel or unnatural to modern readers. Victorian children were meant to be seen, not heard; there was a simple division between right and wrong, and any compromises were attributed to the devil. Sin was to be kept at bay through a mixture of prayer and chastisement, and disciplinary measures were a bulwark against moral waywardness.

It is, of course, possible to exaggerate or overdramatize miserable childhood experiences. In his own memoir, Montgomery's brother Brian rejected the suggestion that their childhood was unhappy or unnatural, claiming, "Bernard did not grow up in an atmosphere of fear—of mother—or develop any inward-looking, withdrawn characteristics because of her."[6] But he also admitted that the domestic regime was strict, with Sunday being devoted to religious observance and an absence of any frivolity, and confirmed the regular imposition of beatings by their mother. On one occasion, young Montgomery was caught smoking—a heinous offense. After his father left the room to pray for his soul, his mother remained to administer a sound thrashing.

While this behavior might not have been any worse than that experienced in a comparable Victorian family, Montgomery's mother seems to have been a martinet who demanded love and obedience through the imposition of a strict moral code. Such an unyielding approach to motherhood was bound to influence her children's upbringing; in this case it left Montgomery with the impression that he had come to "know fear early in life, much too early."[7]

The family's years in Tasmania came to an end in 1901, when Bishop Montgomery was appointed secretary of the Society for the Propagation of the Gospel (SPG), a missionary society established in 1701 to send priests to the British colonies, both to keep the colonists within the Church of England and to convert locals. Bishop Montgomery believed the SPG should be considered as "a sort of Foreign Office" for the creation of international Anglicanism.[8] The work took the family back to London, and, as he had done in Tasmania, the bishop threw himself into the task, believing that through his evangelical efforts he could transform the Church of England into an imperial church with a global reach.

At the age of 14, Montgomery was sent to St. Paul's School in London, a private educational establishment that had been founded in 1509 on a plot of land adjacent to the famous cathedral but had since moved to the suburb of Hammersmith. With its reputation for academic excellence, St. Paul's was one of the country's leading schools with a bias toward the classics, and among its former pupils, or Old Paulines, can be counted the poet John Milton, the Duke of Marlborough, and the diarist Samuel Pepys. Unlike similar schools, such as Cheltenham, Clifton, or Charterhouse, St. Paul's did not have a particularly strong tradition of sending boys into the British army, but after his first day Montgomery announced his intent to join the preparatory class for those wishing to enter either the Royal

Military College, Sandhurst, or the Royal Military Academy at Woolwich. Designated Class C, to denote its relatively low academic standing, its members were considered to be less intellectually gifted, and Montgomery's sudden decision to opt for the army side at St. Paul's caused consternation at home, as his parents had hoped that he would follow a religious vocation.

By then Montgomery was too old to be beaten into submission, and his parents were left to accept their wayward son's decision. They watched helplessly as he refused to participate in the school's academic life. Although he did enough work to pass examinations and showed that he had a retentive mind, he was generally idle and in his memoirs admitted that he did "practically no work" during his time at St. Paul's.[9] As a consequence, punishment by caning on the buttocks was a regular occurrence. Instead of applying himself academically, Montgomery threw himself into athletic activities and emerged as a good player in team sports. He was not physically prepossessing—he stood five feet seven inches tall, with a wiry frame that earned him the nickname of "The Monkey"—but he possessed strength and determination and prospered as a result. In time he became captain of the rugby and cricket teams, and those achievements gave him a high reputation among his peers, who valued grit and sporting achievement. Toward the end of his time at St. Paul's, the school magazine reported that "The Monkey is vicious, of unflagging energy and much feared by the neighbouring animals...to foreign fauna it shows no mercy, stamping on their heads and twisting their necks, and doing many other inconceivable atrocities with a view, no doubt, to proving its patriotism."[10]

All this counted for a great deal in the world Montgomery inhabited. He might not have been a scholar, but he earned respect as a sportsman and a team leader. Without really trying he passed the competitive examinations that took him to Sandhurst in January 1907. His position was 72 out of 170 "gentleman cadets" (as they were termed at the time) admitted that year, but against that could be measured his sporting prowess and leadership abilities. Those attributes stood him in good stead in the early stages of training, and during his first term he was appointed cadet-lance-corporal, his first promotion. But no sooner had Montgomery ascended a few rungs than his career was thrown into doubt following a violent incident with another gentleman cadet. In December 1907, he led his company in an attack on another company's quarters. Matters got out of hand, and during the incident, Montgomery set fire to a fellow cadet's shirttails while he was dressing for dinner. Badly burned, the young man had to be sent to the hospital for medical treatment, and although he refused to name his assailant, the subsequent court of inquiry punished Montgomery, who was reduced to the rank of cadet and sent home in disgrace.

Although boisterous behavior was not discouraged at Sandhurst—there were regular incidents ranging from high spirits to all-out violence—Montgomery had gone beyond the pale by severely injuring a fellow cadet. He was disgraced, his hopes for a military career in ruins, but at that crucial juncture his mother intervened. She arranged to see the college commandant and pleaded her son's case. As a result, young Montgomery was reinstated and returned to Sandhurst in January 1908 to resume his career as a gentleman cadet. Coming from a relatively impecunious family, Montgomery's ambition was to gain a commission in the Indian army, where he would be able to live off his pay and see regular operational service. In an age when British army officers were expected to have private incomes, this was an important consideration.

During the era that Montgomery was being trained as an officer, there was an unofficial pecking order among the regiments of the British army. At the peak were the cavalry regiments and the foot guards, followed by the rifle regiments, the light infantry regiments, the Highland infantry regiments and, in no particular order, the various county regiments. Whatever the regiment, though, every officer needed additional private income, as the annual pay of a second lieutenant—the entry rank—was just over £95 a year ($10,400 today), insufficient to cover even uniform costs and mess bills, which amounted to roughly £10 a month. As late as 1914, the War Office recommended that the minimum needed to survive was £160 a year ($17,600 today), but even that amount meant an abstemious existence for a young officer. Some regiments were more costly than others: officers in cavalry or foot guard regiments had to purchase a variety of uniforms to meet all the variations in service and mess dress, and they were expected to live well in the mess, keeping at least two hunters and three polo ponies. In the late Victorian and Edwardian periods, it was not considered unusual for a smart cavalry regiment to require a young officer to have a private income of up to £1,000 a year ($108,800 today). Far from being a deterrent, the differences in social status implied by the costs were not only understood but accepted by the men involved.

Thus, the Indian army was an attractive option, and as a result only the top gentleman cadets from Sandhurst were considered for a commission. Montgomery was not among them: he passed out 36th in his class, and had to accept his second choice, the Royal Warwickshire Regiment, whose 1st Battalion was serving at Peshawar, near the Khyber Pass in India's North-West Frontier Province. It was not an unreasonable alternative: the Warwicks was a sound county regiment founded in 1675, and at the time it was engaged in operational service along the violent Afghan frontier between Chitral and Baluchistan, where the British sought to maintain control of the strategically important Khyber, Kurram, and Bolan mountain passes.

However, arriving in Peshawar, Montgomery was not impressed by what he found. He arrived during a period of relative quiet and was struck by the insistence on maintaining high social standards within the regiment. Although he continued to excel at sports, he disliked the imperialist social ambience, with its fixation on "good form," and wrote sardonically in his memoirs that "it soon appeared to me that a 'good mixer' was a man who had never been known to refuse a drink."[11] Not only did this lead to a lifelong aversion to alcoholic excess, it left him with a poor opinion of the professionalism of the regiments of the Indian army.

At the end of 1912, Montgomery's battalion returned to England, where it formed part of the 10th Brigade in the 4th Division at Shorncliffe, in Kent. When war broke out against Germany in August 1914, the battalion crossed over to France as part of the British Expeditionary Force (BEF), which had been deployed to support the French Fifth Army on the northern end of the defensive line along the Mons-Conde Canal. This move was part of a prearranged plan by which British forces would support the French flanks in the event of an attack by an enemy country. It was here, rather than in the colonies, that British soldiers' eyes were opened to the realities of modern warfare. The Warwicks first saw action during the confused retreat from Mons to Le Cateau as the BEF pulled back in the face of the German onslaught. The Great Retreat toward the Marne River, as it was known, took the German army to the outskirts of Paris, and the BEF suffered further casualties on August 26, when British II Corps faced the advancing Germans at Le Cateau, some 30 miles from Mons. It was the British army's biggest set-piece battle since Waterloo, in 1815, and its 55,000 soldiers faced Germans numbering 140,000. Lieutenant-General Sir Horace Smith-Dorrien's three divisions, supported by the cavalry division, were able to hold the line by dint of their superior firepower, but by evening they were outnumbered, and only the Germans' failure to press their advantage allowed II Corps to resume their retreat. Even so, the British casualties were heavy—7,812 killed—and gave a stark indication of worse things to come.

For Montgomery it was a sobering experience. He had seen British soldiers retreating in confusion and, worse, witnessed his commanding officer, Lieutenant-Colonel J. F. Elkington, writing a surrender document to prevent the town of Saint-Quentin being destroyed by the advancing Germans. For this action, Elkington was cashiered and dismissed from the British army but later restored his honor as a private soldier in the French Foreign Legion. Montgomery himself evaded capture, but his second battle was almost his last: during the Allied counteroffensive on the Marne, he was shot by a sniper near Meteren, and his wounds in the right lung were so bad that a grave was dug for him. Although he eventually recovered, he was unable to return to frontline service; after a medical board judged that his chest wounds would probably be permanent, he became a staff officer, serving in the training role as brigade major in the 104th Brigade. At the same time, he was awarded the Distinguished Service Order (DSO), a singular honor for a junior officer.

Montgomery was determined to continue his career as a soldier, and early in 1916 his brigade crossed over to France. Despite the severity of his wounds, and even though he had witnessed high casualties in the fighting, Montgomery remained convinced that battles of attrition, such as the Somme in 1916 and Arras and the third battle of Ypres in 1917, were the only way to break German resistance. On July 12, 1916, shortly after the fighting on the Somme began, he wrote to his mother claiming that the men were "wonderfully cheerful" in spite of the heavy losses and the difficult conditions.[12]

By the end of 1917, though, Montgomery's attitude had started to change. Appointed GSO2—staff officer responsible for operations—in IX Corps, he produced a new training manual, a document entitled "Instructions for the Training of Divisions for Offensive Action." It was the first of many such documents that Montgomery would write in the course of his career, and it was created to meet the needs of IX Corps as it prepared for the autumn offensives. The corps was part of the 2nd Army, commanded by General Hubert Plumer, one of the more able British generals of the First World War, who had been responsible for capturing the high ground at Messines in June 1917. With his red face and walrus mustache, Plumer seemed to epitomize the old-fashioned army officer, but in this case appearances were deceptive. He understood that a largely civilian army needed methodical training, and he also believed that battles could only be won with painstaking preparation, ensuring success and minimizing casualties.

Montgomery's training manual for IX Corps reflected many of Plumer's beliefs. The main text was a mere 60 pages, with 40 pages of appendices and 12 pages of maps—a model of cogent simplicity perfectly suited for use by largely untried civilian soldiers. It was basically a blueprint that encouraged the attacking formations to press home their assault under a creeping barrage with fresh units leapfrogging those in the vanguard. Above the battlefield, spotter aircraft would provide aerial reconnaissance and communications, but the emphasis was on solid training and rehearsal so that the assault formations could be optimistic about achieving their objectives. If the men knew what they were doing and were confident about the methods, argued Montgomery, there was no reason why they should not be capable of overcoming the heaviest German defenses.

And so it proved. During the third battle of Ypres (or Passchendaele), Plumer's autumn attacks at Polygon Wood, Menin Road, and Broodseinde succeeded in taking their objectives. In a letter to his mother on November 8, 1917, Montgomery summed up his own philosophy: "The whole art of war is to gain your objective with as little loss as possible."[13] He had almost reached his 30th birthday and was serving in the relatively junior rank of captain at the time, but that declaration of military intent would underpin his attitude to command in the years ahead. In March 1918, Montgomery was made a temporary major and took part in the fighting to contain the huge German offensive in March and April. Conceived at a conference in Mons (held on November 11, 1917, exactly one year before the war would end), the Germans hatched a plan that employed the substantial numbers of German troops, released from the eastern front upon the Russian army's surrender, who could now be used on the western front against the British and French armies. Not only would this give General Erich von Ludendorff a quantitative advantage in the field, but many of the formations were tried-and-tested infantry regiments—Prussians,

Guards, and Swabians—representing the cream of the old German army. Ludendorff's strategy was blunt: his armies would drive a wedge between the two opposing armies, striking through the old Somme battlefield between Arras and La Fère before turning to destroy the British Third and Fifth Armies on the left of the Allied line.

It almost worked. The German offensive took the Allies by surprise, and it was not until the end of April that the sting was taken out of the attack and the line was stabilized following fierce fighting on the Lys River. In July, Montgomery was promoted to lieutenant-colonel and appointed chief staff officer (GSO1) in the 47th (London) Division, commanded by Major-General G. F. Gorringe. Later in life, Montgomery admitted that this experience gave him an introduction to the need for detailed staff work in modern industrialized warfare, and once again he issued a number of pamphlets and directives insisting on strict training before battle and the adhesion to orders during it. Some of the battalion commanders were older and more experienced than Montgomery, but he was clearly respected in his role as the division's principal staff officer. By then, too, it was clear that he had developed a capacity both for reading a battle and for communicating his ideas to others.

With the war entering its final hundred days, the advantage had swung inexorably towards the Allies. Field Marshal Sir Douglas Haig had under his command an army of just under two million men in the field, the largest in Britain's history. And far from being men who were demoralized or battle-weary, morale was high because at long last the balance had tipped their way. They were well trained and well equipped to fight a modern war. This was an army that had grown used to fighting with tanks. It was the first to use predicted shooting; it was the first to develop modern fire-control techniques; it was the first to attack with air support; it was the first to rely on wireless telegraphy for command and control. Above all, the men had confidence in their abilities. When they attacked, they expected to take the enemy's position, and they dared to think that they would come out of the action alive.

Applying relentless pressure, the Allied advance continued throughout October and into November as the Germans steadily retreated from their positions on the western front. Familiar names were retaken—for the British, Le Cateau; for the French, symbolic Sedan, where thousands of lives had been lost in the bitter fighting of 1916. By then the war was as good as over. Turkey capitulated on October 30, bringing to an end the fighting in Mesopotamia and Palestine. Austria-Hungary followed suit on November 3, and things were beginning to fall apart in Germany. Sailors in the Baltic and North Sea ports mutinied after the Germans' High Seas Fleet refused to put to sea for one last battle, and there was civil unrest in Berlin. With revolution looming, Kaiser Wilhelm II had no option but to yield to demands for an armistice.

The following year, on March 24, the 47th Division was disbanded, and Montgomery reverted to his substantive rank of brevet-major. He was 31 and had survived almost five years of intensive warfare; ahead lay an uncertain future.

CHAPTER TWO

Peacetime Soldiering

THE CONCLUSION OF THE GREAT WAR IN NOVEMBER 1918 BROUGHT
THE usual reduction in defense expenditures. Following the construction
of a huge volunteer and conscript army, in the postwar years the Regular
Army returned to its position as a small professional force. Horizons nar-
rowed as regiments returned to business as usual, taking up once again
the familiar patterns and routines of peacetime soldiering. A comatose
condition set in as a bottleneck in promotions led to complacency, and
radical thinking and reform were discouraged. Pacifism arising from the
war's huge death toll was also a disincentive for continued or increased
defense expenditure. All too often, antiwar sentiments became anti–
armed forces sentiments, and the army's image suffered as a result.

For an ambitious young officer like Montgomery, who had distinguished himself in the fighting on the western front, the immediate

postwar period brought considerable challenges. While he had served as a staff officer for most of the conflict, he had not been trained professionally in that role, and when the first lists were published for the army's Staff College at Camberley, his name was not included. Under normal circumstances he might have returned to regimental soldiering, but Montgomery clearly believed that he had to make his own luck. This he did with a single-mindedness that was typical of him throughout his career. Following the disbandment in year 1919 of the 47th Division, he was appointed General Staff Officer, Second Grade (GSO2, Operations) in the general headquarters of the British army on the Rhine, Britain's contribution to the Allied forces occupying Germany. This was a senior staff appointment, and he came into contact with its commander, General Sir William Robertson, who had served as Britain's Chief of the Imperial General Staff (CIGS) between 1915 and 1918 and would later become a field marshal.

"Wully" Robertson was unusual in that he was the first soldier to have risen from the ranks to become a field marshal, an occurrence made all the more remarkable by the fact that he had begun his service as a trooper in an elite cavalry regiment, the 16th Lancers. By dint of hard work and application (he was a good linguist), Robertson rose through the ranks, was commissioned in 1877, and in time became the first ranker to enter the army's Staff College. Throughout his career, he demonstrated a rare professionalism, and his wartime post as CIGS made him one of the most powerful general officers in the post-war army. Robertson's patronage would have been an important factor in any young officer's life, and Montgomery's chance came in the summer of 1919, when he was invited to play tennis at the general's residence in Cologne. Montgomery must have impressed Robertson during the party, because his name appeared on the list for the following year's Staff College intake. At the same time, Montgomery was given temporary command of the 17th Royal Fusiliers, a wartime New Army infantry battalion awaiting disbandment. The appointment lasted only a few months, from September to November 1919.

However, as would happen again and again in his life, the next stage did not live up to expectations, and Staff College turned out to be something of a disappointment. The college was founded in its modern form in 1857 in the aftermath of the disastrous Crimean War of 1854–1856. Its aim was to train bright, young regimental officers in staff work to enable them to carry out the duties of a brigade-major. Entrance was by competitive examination, although, as in Montgomery's case, nomination was also possible for exceptional officers. In the late Victorian period, some British regiments had taken pride in the fact that none of their officers ever attended the college and relied instead on the experience of operational service and regimental soldiering, but the First World War changed that thinking. Ambitious officers began to realize that they had to attend the course in order to ascend the promotion ladder, for carrying the notation *p.s.c.* (passed staff college) on the Army List was an important asset, as indeed it remains today. From the 1920s and into the following decade, six or seven hundred officers applied for a place each year, and a highly competitive examination required candidates to display a broad technical understanding of their profession as well as an intelligent reading of political, economic, strategic, and historical matters. Much of the coursework involved essay writing but teamwork was also important, with groups of officers working in syndicates.

As was the case in the rest of the British army during that period, there was also an emphasis on socializing and demonstrating what was known as "good form." This sort of behavior was no different from the mess life Montgomery had found so distasteful when he first joined the army, but it was also practical: instructors had to assess candidates in a variety of settings and judge their capacity to get on with their brother officers. Field sports might have seemed extraneous, but students' participation in the Staff College Drag Hounds (a popular British hunting sport in which hounds follow a scent over rough ground accompanied by their handlers) allowed instructors to discern their ability to combine mental effort with physical endurance. Although Montgomery relished the opportunity to improve his military education while at Staff College, he kicked against the "gentlemanly" aspects of the course, and he was by his own admission "critical and intolerant" of the instructors and did little to endear himself to them. Contemporary records are sparse, but it seems fair to conclude from the available evidence that during his course Montgomery was conceited, impatient, and opinionated. He was too loquacious for his own good and seemed not to understand the difference between expressing an opinion and listening to opinions expressed by others. Such behavior did not add to his popularity. In the Christmas edition of the college magazine, an anonymous fellow officer posed a question in a column entitled "Things We Want to Know," asking his readers "If and where Monty spent two silent minutes on Armistice Day?"[1]

However, Montgomery's time at Staff College was not altogether wasted. Among his instructors were Lieutenant-Colonel Charles Broad, later deputy director of staff duties at the War Office and author of the influential primer *Mechanised and Armoured Formations* (1929), and John Dill, a future field marshal and Chief of the Imperial General Staff, who would do much to cement the transatlantic alliance during the Second World War. Montgomery may have found certain aspects of the course unsatisfactory and did not apply himself, but it must have done him some good. Although results were never made public, the best candidates were generally given the best appointments—in Montgomery's case, on December 6, 1920, he was appointed brigade-major in the Kerry Infantry Brigade, at the time on operational service in southern Ireland. It was a useful appointment, but a better one followed a week later, when his posting was changed to the larger 17th (Cork) Infantry Brigade in southwest Ireland.

The reason for the presence of British forces in Ireland at this time was the outbreak of the civil war (known variously as the Anglo-Irish War or War of Independence) that preceded independence in 1921. It was a squalid little conflict, with murders and revenge killings carried out by both sides, the Irish Republican Army (IRA) as well as the security forces. "The whole country runs with blood," said an editorial in the *Irish Times* at the time. "Unless it is stopped and stopped soon every prospect of political settlement and material prosperity will perish and our children will inherit a wilderness."[2] Throughout the period of British rule in Ireland, there had been attempts by Irish nationalists to achieve independence, and this latest outbreak had led to renewed hostilities in the immediate postwar period. Despite a huge British military presence, including the use of auxiliaries—usually battle-hardened former soldiers known as "Black and Tans"—the south was in a state of revolutionary ferment, with large tracts of territory under IRA control. The matter was complicated by the presence of Protestant unionists in the north who wanted to remain part of the United Kingdom, and there was a real danger that the entire country could descend into a wider conflict.

For Montgomery, the matter was equally convoluted. He came from a northern Protestant family, and on November 21, 1920, his cousin Lieutenant-Colonel Hugh Montgomery was murdered by the IRA in Dublin while serving as a staff officer at General Headquarters (GHQ) Ireland, one of twelve British officers gunned down that day. (In revenge, the Black and Tans shot an equal number of Irish civilians attending a Gaelic football match at Croke Park in Dublin.) Under those circumstances it would have been excusable if Montgomery had struggled with impartiality, but he showed that he meant business when he took up as his post in January 1921. Probably he had little option. The Cork brigade had seven infantry battalions under its command (in place of the usual three or four), and morale was low, largely because the IRA had started concentrating on attacking British soldiers. Not only was the British army unsuited to fighting an insurgency war of this kind, it lacked useful intelligence and was forced to try to keep the peace while the politicians attempted to find a workable settlement. At the same time, the IRA proved to be a master of guerrilla warfare, operating in small, well-armed "flying columns" and building up support in the southern communities. According to their newspaper *An t-Oglach*, the tactics were to consist of "surprises, ambushes, raids on fortified position and equipment, interruptions of their communications."[3] (This credo would resonate with the Taliban insurgents fighting against Afghan government and NATO forces in Helmand today.)

Reprisals and executions became commonplace as the armed struggle descended into criminality and the Royal Irish Constabulary was unable to contain the insurgents. Acting in their support, the British army was hamstrung, and its policy of sweeps and drives was rarely successful in capturing IRA groups. So, just as he had done with IX Corps, Montgomery produced a set of comprehensive instructions for all British officers serving in Ireland. Emphasis was placed on a disciplined approach to operations and the need to act within the law. Although Montgomery admitted to one of the brigade's intelligence officers, Major A. E. Percival (who would later be named wartime commander of the British forces in Singapore), his own view that a counterinsurgency of this kind could only be won by being ruthless, he acknowledged that "nowadays public opinion precludes such methods." He concluded that the army had to bow to reality and hand the matter over to the Irish and "let them squash the rebellion themselves."[4]

By the summer of 1921, it seemed as though that scenario would be the most likely outcome. A truce followed by the signing of the Anglo-Irish Treaty ended the War of Independence and established the 26 counties of the Irish Free State. The 6 counties of Northern Ireland were allowed to opt out of the agreement and remained under British rule (an arrangement that would cause equally vexing problems into the twenty-first century). A provisional government was established in Dublin, but it was soon at odds with the IRA, whose leadership repudiated the treaty in May 1922. During those last tension-filled days, violence was ever-present and continued as the British army withdrew. One of Montgomery's last actions was an attempt to broker the release of three British officers, one of them an intelligence officer under his command and a member of the Royal Warwickshire Regiment. He was unsuccessful—the bodies were found in a peat bog—but Montgomery's service in Ireland had not gone unnoticed. In April he was appointed brigade-major with the 8th Infantry Brigade based in Plymouth.

It was a useful posting. The brigade was part of 3rd Infantry Division, and its commander, Brigadier-General S. E. Hollond, had a good war record, but Montgomery arrived at a time of cutbacks within the British army. Between 1923 and 1932, the army's budget fell from £43.5 million to £36 million. Equipment was not renewed, and under the Geddes Axe (named after Sir Eric Geddes, chairman of the Committee on National Expenditure), manpower levels were reduced for further savings. By 1920 the army's complement of soldiers had fallen from 3.5 million to 370,000. Under those circumstances, officers had to accept what was offered them—and Montgomery was in no position to complain when he found himself transferred to the 49th (West Riding) Division of the Territorial Army in the role of GSO2. Similar to the United States' National Guard, the Territorial Army had been founded in 1908 as a part-time force for home defense, although most of its battalions and regiments had seen active service on the main fronts of the First World War. Finding himself among part-time soldiers could have seemed like a demotion, but when Montgomery arrived at the division's headquarters at York, he discovered that he could still make opportunities for himself.

As no GSO1 was ever appointed—another casualty of the cutbacks—Montgomery was in effect the division's chief of staff, and he used the opportunity to institute a number of innovations to improve training and efficiency. Once again he turned his hand to producing training pamphlets for the use of officers and noncommissioned officers. Each year Territorial Army divisions attended summer "camps" that lasted two weeks and were supposed to give the part-time soldiers intensive training. Instead of concentrating on drills—the usual procedure—Montgomery used these camps to inculcate tactical and leadership training. He also arranged for officers to use the mess of the local infantry regiment so that they could have a locus for discussion and the exchange of ideas. Those discussions led to the formation of formal training sessions to prepare young officers for the Staff College examination. During this period Montgomery also made a number of enduring friendships with like-minded, forward-looking officers such as Captain (later Sir) Basil Liddell Hart, the outspoken and controversial military theorist, and Captain Francis ("Freddie") de Guingand, who later became his close friend and wartime chief of staff.

After ten years as a staff officer, Montgomery returned to regimental soldiering in March 1925, when he was appointed a company commander in the 1st Royal Warwickshire Regiment at Shorncliffe. He also took over responsibility for the battalion's training program and instituted new methods, in which drills were largely disregarded in favor of fieldcraft, tactics, and realistic battlefield training. Innovations abounded. During one exercise, Montgomery demonstrated the use of Royal Air Force warplanes in support of attacking infantry and practiced night operations. Despite the prevailing economies, live ammunition was used wherever possible.

In the summer of 1925 he received the welcome news that he had been appointed an instructor at Staff College in the rank of brevet lieutenant-colonel, an appointment which he felt put a "hallmark on my Army career."[5] However, one thing was missing from his life. Montgomery was now 38, and his steady rise had given him hope of an early promotion to full lieutenant-colonel and perhaps command of an infantry battalion. But he lacked a wife. Earlier in his career he had argued that young officers should not marry and that celibacy encouraged ambition, but he was fast reaching the age when a wife would be desirable. At the time there was a saying in the British army that subalterns may not marry, captains might marry, majors should marry, and lieutenant-colonels must marry. (Although this was usually said in jest, it did carry a serious message. Not only were junior officers often not sufficiently wealthy to keep a wife, but an early marriage was considered to be deleterious to career prospects.)

However, Montgomery had reached the stage when he must marry, and he determined that he should find a wife. In the previous summer, he had become infatuated with Betty Anderson, the 18-year-old daughter of an official in the Indian Civil Service, and although she had rejected his advances, he decided to push his suit once more, traveling to Switzerland where the Andersons were on vacation.

Once again, though, he was rebuffed by Betty Anderson. But the visit was not wasted, as Montgomery met another woman who attracted him—Betty Carver, née Hobart, the widow of a soldier killed during the Gallipoli campaign in 1915, who had two sons, aged 11 and 13. Like him, she came from an Irish background, and her brothers were army officers—one of whom had been in Montgomery's course at Staff College six years earlier. What began as a close friendship blossomed into love, and they married in London on July 27, 1927. Montgomery took over responsibility for bringing up Betty's two sons, and in the following year she gave birth to their only son together, David.

Earlier, Montgomery had agreed with his contemporaries that marriage was an impediment, but he soon discovered that it had little bearing on his capabilities. As an instructor at Camberley, he emerged as an exceptional lecturer who seemed to have an intuitive feeling for warfare and was able to convey his ideas to his students, many of whom were destined to serve under his command in the Second World War. He was also influenced by the college's director of studies, Colonel Alan Brooke, an artillery officer who would be CIGS during the Second World War. An exponent of armored warfare, Brooke, like Montgomery, believed that senior officers should take an inclusive approach by mastering command of infantry and armored formations. Later, this thinking would be central to the conduct of land operations during the Second World War, especially when the Allies had to counter the threat of German armored warfare. This period, too, honed Montgomery's thinking on modern warfare. He argued in his regiment's magazine, "It seems that the time is coming when the tanks will be the assault arm of the army, the artillery will be the arm which makes the assault possible, and the infantry the arm which occupies the conquered area."[6]

At the end of 1928, Montgomery's period as an instructor came to an end, and he returned to his regiment as a company commander. As there was little work for him to do when he arrived at the battalion's headquarters in Woking, the War Office appointed him secretary of a committee that was revising the *Infantry Training Manual, Volume II*. It was published in 1930, and although it was criticized by Liddell Hart—who believed that Montgomery had failed to emphasize the use of reserves to exploit a successful attack—the manual is noteworthy for its straightforward and unadorned style. Equally important, it added to Montgomery's reputation within the army, as the manual laid down the tactical doctrine to be followed by regimental infantry officers. The following year, he went back to the battalion as second-in-command and then took it over when it was deployed to Palestine in January of 1931.

For any regimental officer, the moment of assuming command of a battalion is a high-water mark in his career. This is especially true in the British army, where infantry and cavalry regiments are considered to be as much families as fighting formations. Attachments ran deep: a disagreement within the regiment would be quickly resolved and forgotten, but any insult from outside, real or imagined, would be fiercely repulsed. Soldiers took pride in the fact that they had inherited history and traditions from past wars and campaigns. It was no different in Montgomery's Royal Warwickshire Regiment. It was one of 25 senior infantry regiments in the British army's order of battle, with two regular battalions: one for home service, the other for overseas operations. Under an arrangement begun as a result of reforms instituted in 1881, the home service battalion generally undertook training of recruits and provided regular drafts for the battalion serving overseas.

When Montgomery took over command of 1st Royal Warwickshire Regiment, it had been the home service battalion since the end of the First World War, but now it was about to change places with the 2nd

Battalion, which had been serving in India, and latterly, in Sudan. For the men involved, it was an unsettling period. Ahead lay up to 21 years of overseas service, first in Palestine and Egypt and then in India. Older men coming to the end of their service were exempted from the tour of duty, which meant that Montgomery not only took over command of a depleted battalion of four hundred but had to take drafts from the returning 2nd Battalion, many of whose members were unhappy not to be going home. On top of the natural turbulence always involved in a change of command—the previous two commanding officers had been highly regarded—Montgomery found himself taking an unhappy group of men to a not particularly popular posting where wives were not permitted to accompany the battalion for the first year.

◈

Palestine had come under British control in 1920 as a mandated territory of the League of Nations, and Article Six states that "the Administration of Palestine, while ensuring that the rights and position of other sections of the population are not prejudiced, shall facilitate Jewish immigration under suitable conditions." By this agreement Britain kept its wartime promise (in the Balfour Declaration of 1917) to provide "a national home for the Jewish people" while safeguarding the interests of the resident Arab population. It did not turn out that way, however, and during the 1920s and 1930s, there was constant friction between the local Arab population and the incoming Jews. Two years before Montgomery's arrival, there were serious Arab disturbances in Hebron, resulting in 69 Jews being killed and hundreds wounded, but during the battalion's year in Palestine, the mood was reasonably tranquil.

This was more than could be said about what was happening within Montgomery's battalion. Apart from the natural distrust of their new, relatively unknown leader, the regiment was offended when Montgomery instituted a new system of promotion whereby noncommissioned officers would be promoted not according to length service but to merit, a system which was eventually adopted by the British army and is still in use today. The change was unwelcome in the sergeants' mess, traditionally the backbone of any infantry battalion, and for a while, morale plummeted. On the other hand, the men responded well to Montgomery's training programs. But those first months in command were likely not easy for a man who was used to getting his own way. It did not help matters that Montgomery was the senior officer in Palestine reporting to the General Officer Commanding (GOC) Egypt and Palestine, whose headquarters was in distant Cairo, and Montgomery had perforce to spend time away from his battalion. But he must have done some things correctly, as the GOC's personal report on him in March 1932 complimented Montgomery as "clever, energetic, ambitious, and a very good instructor." His shortcomings included a lack of "tact, tolerance, and discretion," but by any standards it was a good report.[7]

At the beginning of 1932, the battalion transferred to a new station at Alexandria in Egypt. During its stay Montgomery added to his growing reputation as a superior tactical instructor by introducing night training and demonstrating a boldness of approach that brought him plaudits from senior officers. He also caused something of a sensation by introducing a battalion brothel, which was regularly inspected by the medical officers, for soldiers wishing to take part in what Montgomery called "horizontal refreshment." He abolished compulsory attendance at church parades and continued to de-emphasize drill, which he believed only improved a soldier's ability to march and did little to prepare him for the shock of battle.

Two years later, at the end of 1933, the battalion was on the move once more, this time to India, where its new station was at Poona (present-day Pune), which had the reputation of being the spiritual home of the British army in India. It also had a reputation, not altogether undeserved, as representing the more snobbish and class-bound side of British rule in India. Not for nothing was Poona known as the "sloth belt." It was not to Montgomery's liking, but relief came at the beginning of 1934, when he was appointed chief instructor at the Indian Staff College at Quetta (in present-day Pakistan) and to the rank of full colonel. As the college was on a par with Camberley and attracted officers from India and the Dominions, this was a key appointment, and Montgomery immediately sought to make a good impression on his superiors. Within a year the college commandant, Major-General Guy Williams, recommended him for promotion to command a brigade, and this came to pass in February 1937, when Montgomery was given command of the 9th Infantry Brigade at Portsmouth. On leaving, Williams's personal report described him as "an outstanding officer" who was set to go far in the army.[8]

CHAPTER THREE

The Drift to War

IN EARLY SUMMER 1937, MONTGOMERY ARRIVED BACK IN ENGLAND, and in August, after an extended leave, he took command of the 9th Infantry Brigade at a time when it was due to take part in exercises on Salisbury Plain. The brigade consisted of four infantry battalions: the 2nd Queen's Royal Regiment, the 2nd Middlesex Regiment, the 1st King's Own Scottish Borderers, and the 2nd Lincolnshire Regiment. It formed part of the 3rd Infantry Division under the direction of the Southern Command, whose General Officer Commanding (GOC) was General John Burnett-Stuart, previously Montgomery's overall commander in Egypt and Palestine. Montgomery, as usual, wasted little time in imposing himself on his new command. Previous plans for the exercise were torn up, and he instituted a more rigorous approach, with longer operations lasting up to three days and the introduction of more-realistic tactical plans. The culmination of the exercise was the defeat of a rival brigade using an indirect flanking attack and taking it by surprise.

Once again Montgomery's star was ascending, but it was at this propitious moment that disaster struck. While the Montgomerys' official residence was being redecorated in Portsmouth, Betty took their son David for a seaside holiday at Burnham-on-Sea in Somerset. It should have been a carefree time, but on the first day Betty's foot was bitten by an unknown insect on the beach, and the wound immediately became infected. At first the wound was treated as inflammation, but as the summer gave way to autumn, it became clear that she was seriously unwell. Hers proved to be a long-lingering illness, and as the blood-poisoning spread, the decision was taken to amputate the infected leg. Six weeks later, on October 19, she succumbed to pneumonia and died in her husband's arms. The cause of death was recorded as septicemia, but neither the identity of the insect nor the reason for the onset of blood poisoning was ever discovered.

Montgomery was shattered. He had been deeply in love with Betty, and now he had to face the future without her, as well as accept the responsibility for bringing up their nine-year-old son. His way of dealing with the tragedy was not to surrender to grief but to fight it. As soon as the postmortem was concluded, Montgomery arranged for his wife's body to be buried at Burnham-on-Sea, even though there was no particular connection with the place. The burial was attended only by Montgomery, his brigade-major, a staff captain, the driver of his staff car, and the officiating priest, Canon Dick Sheppard. That same night he drove himself back to Portsmouth, and two days later he told his stepson Dick that he doubted if he would ever get over Betty's death.

Viewed from our present day and age, Montgomery's response to his wife's passing might seem unfeeling, even unnatural. To a certain extent it was, but it should be judged in the context of his time and his own emotional makeup. Montgomery belonged to a generation that believed emotions should be mastered, and he had come through a war in which self-sacrifice in the national cause was often considered to be an inspiring example to others. Perhaps, too, he believed that he had to bear the pain of Betty's loss with the same stoicism as he had endured beatings as a child. And like others who have lost loved ones, he would have wondered what he could have done to avoid the tragedy. However, none of those nostrums were of any immediate use to him, and Montgomery went back to his work knowing that his life would never be the same again. Some have suggested that Montgomery might have emerged "a deeper, richer human being" if he had grieved longer and allowed himself time to readjust to what had happened.[1] As it was, he was back at his desk almost immediately. He threw himself into his duties, displaying the same indomitable energy that had marked his earlier career. It was a time of great turbulence, not just in international politics, but also within the army.

Two years earlier, Stanley Baldwin had returned to power as prime minister of the coalition National Government, which was now committed to addressing the problem of imperial defense. Although there was little public support for increased expenditure, steps were taken to improve air defenses and to bolster naval strength for the protection of vital trading routes. Even the army, long ignored, received new resources. The new secretary of war was Isaac Leslie Hore-Belisha, whose goal was to bring change to the army, or, as he put it, to make senior officers believe that "the Army should be a part of the nation and not apart from the nation."[2] Possessed of a flamboyant personality and a gift for self-promotion, Hore-Belisha instituted a process of rapid reforms to increase pay, modernize barrack conditions, and improve the soldiers' career structure. Although the innovations won him a reputation as "the soldier's friend," he also made enemies, and his selection of Field Marshal Lord Gort as CIGS was not welcomed by everyone. John Vereker, the sixth viscount of Gort, was another of the army's many distinguished Irish soldiers and had won a Victoria Cross (Britain's highest award for valor) while commanding the 3rd Guards Brigade in 1918. In the postwar years he had been employed in a variety of staff jobs but never mastered the art of military politics; as a result, he was soon at odds with Hore-Belisha's reforms.

✛

All the while, the situation in Europe was deteriorating, and the British government seemed supine and muddled in its response. Adolf Hitler had come to power in Germany in 1934 and had quickly established a Nazi dictatorship, whose aim was to re-arm the country's forces and to dismantle the Treaty of Versailles. Conscription was brought back, and in 1936 the German army reoccupied the Rhineland, the buffer zone between France and Germany. At the same time Benito Mussolini, the Fascist dictator of Italy, began a program of expansionism that the other European countries were powerless to check. The first flashpoint came in 1938, when Austria was coerced into joining forces with Germany (the Anschluss). Next, Hitler made territorial demands on the new republic of Czechoslovakia by threatening to annex Sudetenland, home to 14 million Germans. Although war was averted at Munich by the intervention of British prime minister Neville Chamberlain, Baldwin's successor, it was only a pause for breath. A new European war was on the horizon, and Britain belatedly began preparing for the outbreak of hostilities.

During this period, Hore-Belisha changed his priorities from defense of the homeland, especially from aerial attack, to the creation of a field force capable of fighting in Europe. New equipment started arriving (albeit late and in miserly numbers), the size of the Territorial Army was doubled, and conscription was introduced for the first time in peacetime. In the summer of 1938, Montgomery persuaded the GOC's 3rd Division that the summer's exercises should involve an amphibious assault supported by naval strike aircraft at Slapton Sands in Devon. He would not know how important this exercise would prove to be in the long run. Although it was successful, it also revealed the need for landing craft: Montgomery's three assault battalions came ashore in naval cutters, just as their predecessors had done at the Gallipoli landings in 1915—and for that matter, just as James Wolfe's infantrymen had done at Quebec in 1759 during the Seven Years' War (1756–1763), during the British attempt to oust the French from Canada. Following the exercise, Montgomery was given responsibility for creating British army doctrine for the defensive and protective measures to be used in the event of gas attacks. The resultant Trial Report was highly praised and remained in use throughout the Second World War.

In October 1938 Montgomery was offered the command of the 8th Infantry Division and a promotion to the rank of major-general. On one hand, he might have preferred staying with his brigade, as the 3rd Division was one of the groups earmarked to form part of the British Expeditionary Force, or BEF, in the event of a war with Germany. However, his new command would take him back to Palestine, by then in a state of turmoil, with tensions running high between the Arab and Jewish populations. Despite his steady success, Montgomery had already been overlooked for several earlier promotions, he could not afford to be choosy. So he went to Palestine, which brought him under the command of General Sir Archibald Wavell, considered to be one of the army's rising stars and who, like Montgomery, enjoyed a reputation as a superb trainer of troops. As GOC Middle East, Wavell's responsibilities and territories were vast, stretching from Palestine to Egypt and including Sudan, Cyprus, British Somaliland, Aden, Iraq, and the Persian Gulf. It was at Wavell's insistence that command of the 8th Infantry Division, based at Haifa, was given to Montgomery. In a year-end report on Montgomery, his new commander described him as "one of the clearest brains we have in the higher ranks," although he also noted that Montgomery suffered from "some of the defects of the enthusiast, in an occasional impatience and intolerance when things cannot be done as quickly as he would like."[3]

In other respects, however, Palestine was not an ideal posting: Arab protests against continuing Jewish immigration had spiraled into violence in 1936, as both sides attacked each other and the British security forces were caught in the middle. A commission headed by Lord

William Peel recommended that the country should be partitioned and Jewish immigration limited to 12,000 a year, but this news only exacerbated the violence. Further conferences failed to find resolution. With the European situation worsening, Britain issued a White Paper (a British parliamentary paper setting out policy proposals for wider discussion) in May 1939 that provided for a limitation of Jewish immigration to 75,000 over the next five years and the establishment "within ten years of an independent Palestine State in such treaty relations with the United Kingdom as will provide for all commercial and strategic interests on both countries."[4] Needless to say, neither side was prepared to accept such an outcome—not the Arabs, because they would be in a minority, and not the Jews, because it seemed to be a betrayal of the 1917 Balfour Declaration. Brokered by the British foreign secretary A. J. Balfour and Lord Rothschild, the leader of the British Jewish community, the declaration stated that in return for financial support from the international Zionist community during the war, Britain would use its best efforts to provide them with a national home in Palestine.

It was against that uneasy background that Montgomery arrived in Palestine to take over command of his new division whose area of responsibility included Samaria, Galilee, and the northern border with Syria. It was not promising territory. The names contained echoes from the Old Testament and little appeared to have changed since biblical times. Roads were often primitive, much of the land was semidesert and only roughly cultivated, and the infrastructure was fairly basic. On arrival Montgomery inspected the division's 35 outposts, as well as police posts and Jewish settlements under British protection. He quickly concluded that the main tasks were protection of the local population, destruction of rebel Arab gangs, and training the local police to take over the responsibilities of the British army.

Today this has a familiar ring. Following the 2003 invasion of Iraq and the overthrow of President Saddam Hussein, the U.S.-led coalition forces had to evolve similar tactics to cope with an insurgency led by former members of the Baathist regime and other groups opposed to the invasion, and it was not until 2007 that the violence was brought under control with methods that had been used 70 years earlier in Palestine. It was (and remains) a classic counterinsurgency doctrine, and Montgomery had learned it from his earlier experiences in Ireland fighting the IRA. However, he took the application further by insisting that the Arabs did not form a national movement but were simply criminal gangs to be quashed and their adherents punished. In fact, the Arabs were under the direction of the Arab Higher Committee led by Haj Amin al-Husseini, the mufti of Jerusalem, but Montgomery's instincts were correct. For all intents and purposes, British forces in Palestine were involved in a state of open war against a largely hidden enemy. In a series of letters to headquarters in Jerusalem written in the early months of 1939, Montgomery insisted that the army's primary responsibility was the suppression of the revolt and the restoration of law and order and that, therefore, there should be no diminution of British forces in Palestine.

The correspondence sheds an interesting light on Montgomery's methods. Not only does it demonstrate his firm grip on the security situation within Palestine, it also provides sensible solutions. Above all, it was very much to the point: he criticized the existing situation, especially the condition of the Palestinian Police Force, which he condemned as "useless," a favorite pejorative he used in reports and correspondence to describe individuals and organizations that failed to meet his standards. By then, though, events in Palestine were taking second place to the deepening crisis in Europe, where German forces invaded Czechoslovakia in March 1939 and Hitler entered into a "Pact of Steel" with Mussolini. War now seemed inevitable.

In April, Montgomery was warned by the military secretary at the War Office to prepare to return to Britain to take over command of the 3rd Infantry Division, which had been formed in 1809 by the Duke of Wellington to fight in the French in the Iberian Peninsula (1808–1814) and was nicknamed, variously, the "Fighting Third," the "Iron Division," or "Ironsides"—the last an allusion to the name given to Oliver Cromwell's force during the seventeenth-century English Civil

War. Montgomery was keen to assume command before the agreed-on date of October 1, but no sooner had he responded to the order than he was stricken with a mysterious illness. It began as a fever and developed into pleurisy (an infection of the lungs), and there were soon fears that he was suffering from a tubercular infection. The medical staff was unable to make an accurate diagnosis, and despite his difficulty in breathing, Montgomery decided that he should return home immediately. A long voyage with sea air and plenty of rest might seem like a medical cliché for a cure, but in Montgomery's case it worked. When he arrived back in London and was treated at the Queen Alexandra military hospital in Millbank, he was given a clean bill of health, and there was no sign of infection. Although the subsequent medical board passed him as fit, there was a hiatus while arrangements were made for Montgomery to take over command of the 3rd Division, and it was not until August 28 that he arrived at its headquarters in Portsmouth. A week later Britain was at war with Nazi Germany.

Under the circumstances, Montgomery had very little opportunity to turn the division into an efficient fighting formation capable of taking its place in the British Expeditionary Force by the time it crossed over to France. With 4th Infantry Division (Major-General D. G. Johnson VC), it formed II Corps, commanded by Lieutenant-General Sir Alan Brooke. Contrary to expectation, command of the BEF was given to Gort, whose place as CIGS was given to General Sir Edmund Ironside (a well-known and highly decorated soldier thought to be the model for John Buchan's fictional character Richard Hannay, the hero of *The Thirty-Nine Steps* and other novels). On September 29, with no road transport and little opportunity for weapons training, the division landed at Cherbourg, only to find that its transport was hundreds of miles away at Brest.

It was an inauspicious start, and worse followed when the division deployed to its first position south of Lille, where the only defense consisted of a single antitank ditch. This frustrating period lasted until May 1940 and came to be known as the "phony war" when both sides considered their options in Western Europe following the rapid collapse of Poland. The German plan called for the invasion of the Low Countries using two army groups to smash through the southern Netherlands and central Belgium while making a diversionary attack through the Ardennes. The ultimate goal of this so-called *Fall Gelb* (Plan Yellow) was to gain control of the Channel ports as a prelude to invading Britain. However, Hitler prevaricated, the plans were subjected to constant change, and there were delays in correcting the balance of ground forces. At the same time the French dithered and ordered an unnecessary move into the Saarland, which did nothing to alter the strategic balance in the Allies' favor and brought only demoralization and defeatism. As for the British, they eventually deployed 13 infantry divisions (5 Regular, 8 Territorial) in France, but of these only the Regular divisions (including Montgomery's), were equipped with tracked Bren gun carriers and modern 25-pound field guns, as well as 2-pound antitank guns. Other improvements included the supply of 3-inch mortars and the new Boys antitank rifle. Only gradually were the other Territorial divisions similarly equipped—and frequently too late. But regardless of weaponry, and as the 3rd Division's historian made clear, everything hung on the readiness of the men: "The soldiers who made up the Division were disciplined, cheerful and a blend of youth and maturity—young Regulars waiting to join their overseas battalions and rejoined Reservists who had completed seven years' colour service."[5]

There was no armor and precious little air cover for Montgomery's men, and this would be a serious shortcoming given the open terrain in northern France and Belgium, where the Germans also had access to a modern system of roads. Compared to the Luftwaffe's 4,200 warplanes, the Allies possessed only 2,000, half of which were fighters. The German machines were also superior in qualitative terms, and their air crews enjoyed better training and tactics (the Royal Air Force wisely held back its valuable, modern Spitfire fighters for the defense of the British homeland). The absence of Allied armored and air support gave the Germans a big advantage, and to counter it Montgomery began training his division in mobile operations in advance of a proposed move toward the Belgian border with its water obstacles provided by the Scheldt, Escaut, and Dyle rivers and their canals. He was also realistic enough to draw up plans for a possible withdrawal. Using the attention to detail that had worked so well in the past, he produced comprehensive orders for the first field exercises at the end of October. They lasted four days and included training for movement by night, the creation of enhanced divisional communications and, above all, the instillation of a common will to win, no matter the odds stacked against them. During this period, Montgomery made sure that he was known to as many of his men as possible by visiting frontline units and talking to soldiers of all ranks, constantly interrogating them about their training and their role. Among the officers it became an instant custom to attempt to ask a question that he could not answer. It never worked.

By then it was clear that German indecisiveness precluded any immediate attack, but Brooke insisted that training should continue and that steps should be taken immediately by the two divisions to improve their defense in depth. On November 1, 1939, he wrote in his diary that while it was unlikely that the Germans would invade Belgium that year, his forces had to train as if they were on the point of doing just that. The entry also shows that he took a good deal of interest in what Montgomery and Johnston were doing and was always ready to offer suggestions for improvement:

> We are not yet out of the woods but the probability of such an eventuality is distinctly less. Even should an attack materialise now we are in a much better situation to meet it than at the beginning of October. However we still require months of training with the necessary facilities, such as artillery and anti-tank ranges, before this Corps can be considered as fit for war. Spent the day touring round the artillery defences of the front, and am not happy with them. Positions are too far back and liaison between infantry and artillery inadequate. Shall see Monty about this tomorrow.[6]

Training continued into the winter months, and throughout this period Montgomery insisted on the maintenance of high standards and a strict adhesion to his written orders. Weak or "useless" commanders were sacked if they failed to inspire confidence in their men or revealed themselves as being insufficiently mentally robust, and on this point Montgomery was ruthless. "Train hard and fight easy" became the division's credo, and it was to stand them in good stead as winter gave way to spring, the change in weather enhancing the threat of a German attack. Hitler had intended to launch the invasion of France as early as mid-November, but the onset of winter had hindered armored operations, and in January 1940 the plans had to be changed again when a copy fell into Allied hands. A new plan, code-named *Sichelschnitt* (Sickle Stroke), changed the weight of the attack to the south, where Army Group A would attack through the rugged and supposedly impenetrable forests of the Ardennes before racing north to the Channel ports.

To counter the threat, the Allied supreme commander, the French general Maurice-Gustave Gamelin, had produced Plan D, which would see 33 British and French divisions moving eastward to invade Belgium as soon as the German attack began. Once on Belgian territory they would take up station along the Dyle Line—a defensive position that ran along the Dyle River to Wavre. At the last minute it was extended north to Breda and the Maas River, the idea being to present the Germans with a defensive line that ran from Antwerp to the heavily fortified Maginot Line at Longuyon. On the outbreak of hostilities it was agreed that Montgomery's 3rd Division would spearhead II Corps when it moved 60 miles into Belgium toward the Dyle Line—by then Brooke also had the 50th (Northumberland) Division, a Territorial formation, under his command.

War came to the BEF with a vengeance on May 10, 1940, when the Germans subjected France to the frightening tactics of blitzkrieg, using armor and airpower to back a rapid ground assault into Belgium, Luxembourg, and the Netherlands. The surprise was total and resistance was negligible. Early in the morning German airborne units of Army Group B began landing in the Netherlands to capture The Hague and the vital crossings of the Meuse. Two days later all Dutch resistance was at an end as the country capitulated. In Belgium the fortress of Eben Emael was soon in German hands even though it was thought to be impregnable. And as the Dutch forces fell back toward Rotterdam and Amsterdam they left the Belgian left flank unprotected. At the same time seven German panzer divisions of German Army Group A pushed through the Ardennes and began their unexpected move toward the Channel ports.

While this was happening, the BEF made their prearranged move into Belgium toward the Dyle Line, passing well-known battlefields of earlier wars—Waterloo, Ypres, Mons. Even at that stage Gort was confident that the Germans could be held, issuing an order of the day on May 13, telling his troops that "the struggle will be hard and long, but we can be confident of final victory."[7] Montgomery was less sure after finding a demoralized Belgian division at Louvain and ordered his to dig in for its defense. Despite the imminent danger, he was in his element—not least because he believed that he had done everything possible to make his men fit for battle and that they were ready, as he said, "to be bloodied." In his memoirs he left an account of the way he himself prepared for the shock of battle, a regime he would follow for the rest of the war:

> It was during this campaign that I developed the habit of going to bed early, soon after dinner. I was out and about on the front all day long, saw all my subordinate commanders, and heard their problems and gave decisions and verbal orders. I was always back at my divisional HQ about teatime, and would see my staff and give orders for the night and the next day. I would then have dinner and go to bed, and was never to be disturbed except in a crisis.[8]

The catastrophe came sooner than expected, on May 16, when Gort decided to retreat toward the Escaut Canal following the collapse of Belgian forces on the BEF's flanks. It was a time of considerable confusion, but after visiting the headquarters of the 3rd Division, Brooke was cheered to find Montgomery "completely unaffected by the seriousness of the situation," and he left with the belief that the withdrawal would be a "complete success." As Montgomery admitted at the time, it was a tricky operation, but within a week Brooke was prepared to admit that "nothing but a miracle can save the BEF and the end cannot be very far off."[9] By then tentative plans had been laid for evacuation as the BEF disengaged from the enemy and began pulling back toward the Channel. These were then firmed up on May 25, when Gort postponed a proposed counterattack to the south and ordered the evacuation of the BEF at Dunkirk.

Later, in his book *The Path to Leadership,* Montgomery praised Gort for acting with "courage and decision," saving the British Army and allowing it to fight another day even though it had to leave the bulk of its heavy equipment on the beaches.[10] The evacuation at Dunkirk is one of the great feats in British military history, and even though it was achieved with the help of German indecision and the Luftwaffe's inability to block the operation, it was still a huge success. Winston Churchill, who had become prime minister on May 10, was careful to say that "wars are not won by evacuations,"[11] but it remains a fact that 338,226 British service personnel were plucked from defeat and capture by the Germans between May 26 and June 3 during the fighting retreat and hurried evacuation. In that sense at least, it was a triumph of sorts.

Inevitably, not everyone behaved well. Later stories emerged of soldiers being threatened at gunpoint and of sailors using their oars as clubs to prevent small boats from being swamped, but most of the regular formations remained disciplined and under control. One of the best in that respect was Montgomery's 3rd Division, which carried out a meticulous nighttime retreat toward the Dunkirk perimeter following plans laid down and practiced earlier in the campaign. "It was a task that might have shaken the stoutest of hearts," noted Brooke, "but for Monty it might just have been a glorious picnic!"[12]

Thanks to Montgomery's planning and the soldiers' discipline, the 3rd Division reached the Dunkirk beaches with 13,000 men. When Brooke was ordered back to London to help reform a new army for further service in France, Montgomery took over temporary command of II Corps. On the morning of June 1, he himself was evacuated on board the destroyer HMS *Codrington,* which was heavily bombed during the short voyage to Dover. Montgomery marked his return in his diary with the terse words: "Arrived London 15.00 hours and reported to CIGS at War Office."[13]

CHAPTER FOUR

Full of Binge

MONTGOMERY RETURNED FROM DUNKIRK TO FIND THE ARMED FORCES and their senior commanders in a state of muddle bordering on catatonia. While there was widespread relief that the British Expeditionary Force (BEF) had been evacuated, and in some circles the operation was being hailed as some kind of victory, no one in the higher reaches of the command structure seemed to know what to do next. By then Field Marshal Sir John Dill had replaced Edmund Ironside as Chief of the Imperial General Staff (CIGS), and John Gort remained in command of the BEF at least until he had finished writing up his dispatches. At the same time Brooke was given command of a second BEF numbering a projected 200,000 troops, which attempted to bolster the remaining French forces in Normandy as they battled halfheartedly to contain the German invasion. This latter operation lasted less than a fortnight, and by the middle of June all British regular forces had retired from France.

Montgomery was also on the move. He returned to command the 3rd Infantry Division, which was first held in general reserve on the south coast of England and then given responsibility for organizing combined service operations. In rapid succession Montgomery received contradictory and bewildering orders to plan for the invasion of the Azores, the Cape Verde Islands, and then the Irish Republic, in case the Germans attempted to seize Cork and the port of Cobh (Queenstown). All three orders were countermanded soon after they were issued—much to Montgomery's disgust—because even at that early stage he believed that it was vital to instigate offensive, rather than merely defensive, operations against the enemy.

It was a curious time. The possibility of invasion remained a potent threat, and the southern counties along the Channel coast became a huge armed camp. However, no precise plans had ever been laid to counter an invasion, as the last serious attempt had taken place in February 1797, when a small French force had landed at Fishguard in Wales during the war against revolutionary France. It was the precursor of a larger invasion force, but it was quickly subdued and rounded up. The Irish rebel Wolfe Tone, who supported the action, described the rebels as "unmitigated blackguards"; and in one instance, a dozen French soldiers surrendered to a Welsh woman armed only with a pitchfork in the mistaken belief that her traditional red cloak denoted that she was a soldier. Half a century later, during the reign of Napoleon III, there was another scare, but in Montgomery's day the possibility of any invasion actually taking place was so remote that it had never been considered by the army's Staff College.

All that changed in the summer of 1940, when it seemed probable that Hitler's victorious army would launch a cross-Channel attack from France, using their more powerful air force to pave the way by destroying the Royal Air Force's fighter bases in the southern counties. The planned response was a mixture of solid military planning to deter a threat that was all too real and outbursts of hysteria about clandestine enemy guerrilla forces and the likelihood of attacks by German airborne forces. Montgomery put his division on a war footing and instituted a program of hard training. All leave was cancelled—a move which was vastly unpopular with the soldiers under his command—and steps were taken to secure the local area between the seaside towns of Brighton and Bognor Regis. An order in the divisional war diary gives some idea of Montgomery's thorough but perhaps overzealous approach in dealing with a densely populated area:

> The Divisional Commander said we had now got to the stage where we must do what we like as regards upsetting private property. If a house was required as an HQ it must be taken. Any material required to improve the defences should be taken. On matters of this nature unit commanders must decide for themselves and must not decentralise. Kindness, firmness and politeness was all that was required.[1]

Although Montgomery's sense of urgency matched the seriousness of the hour, his approach was not always popular. At the time, six infantry divisions had been allotted to guard the Channel coastline between Dover in Kent and Lyme Bay in Dorset, but Montgomery argued that because his 3rd Division had returned almost intact from Dunkirk and was properly trained in mechanized warfare, it should be used as a mobile reserve. He put his case to Winston Churchill when the prime minister inspected British beach defenses at the beginning of July. Not only did Montgomery argue for a more offensive role, he astonished Churchill during dinner by abstaining from alcohol, telling him that he neither drank nor smoked and was 100 percent fit. As Montgomery remembered later, Churchill "replied in a flash that he both drank and smoked and was 200 percent fit." However, the prime minister was impressed by Montgomery's thinking, and as a result of the meeting the 3rd Division was given a mobile offensive counterattack role in the event of a German invasion.[2] This was not dissimilar to the policy evolved by the commander of V Corps, Lieutenant-General Claude Auchinleck, who had decided to concentrate his available forces on beach defense with a number of continuous defensive lines—or stop lines—to counter any German breakthrough. These would be manned by armored forces, which Auchinleck hoped would deal the German invaders a "knockout blow."

Auchinleck agreed with Montgomery that the "lack of a mobile reserve is serious" and warned that there were dangers in having "all our goods in the front window," but he remained adamant that defense of the beaches should be his first priority. He also shared with Montgomery the belief that the Territorial soldier could be as good as his Regular counterpart, and there was an urgent need to integrate the forces. "We shall not win this war so long as we cling to worn-out shibboleths and snobberies," Auchinleck told Lieutenant-General Sir Robert Haining, the new Vice Chief of the Imperial General Staff. "I am sure of this. Cobwebs want removing at once."[3]

Montgomery, though, was not impressed by Auchinleck, whom he seemed to dislike instinctively. Both men were about the same age—Auchinleck was Montgomery's senior by three years—and both had served in the First World War. Both had experience of battle and had acquitted themselves well. Auchinleck had fought in the Mesopotamian campaign of 1915–1918 when a joint British-Indian army had invaded the Ottoman province (later Iraq) to secure its vital oil fields, and more recently he had commanded the British forces in the ill-fated expedition to Narvik, in Norway. "The Auk" (as he was known throughout the army) was a tough-minded fighting soldier and the two men had much in common, but Montgomery revealed in his memoirs that they could never agree on anything. Perhaps Montgomery's dislike was fueled by his distrust of the Indian army—after leaving Sandhurst Auchinleck joined the 62nd Punjabi Regiment—or perhaps it was simply a clash of personalities. For his part, Auchinleck never bore any grudge against Montgomery, but the enmity was unfortunate, as both men's paths would cross again later in the war.

In July 1940, shortly after becoming prime minister, Churchill altered the command structure for the defense of the United Kingdom when he fired Ironside as commander in chief of the home forces and replaced him with Alan Brooke. In the shakeup Auchinleck was promoted to full general and became GOC Southern Command while Montgomery replaced him as commander of V Corps in the rank of lieutenant-general. Both these appointments were well merited, but the changes simply exacerbated Montgomery's dislike of his predecessor. No sooner had Montgomery taken over command of V Corps than he delivered a scathing assessment of its capabilities and of the defensive tactics evolved by Auchinleck. A number of commanders deemed by Montgomery to be "useless" were removed from their positions and a series of adverse reports quickly arrived on Auchinleck's desk. As the Auk had made the appointments in the first place, it must have been a tense start to the new relationship.

Worse followed later in the summer when Montgomery made a direct approach to the adjutant-general (the War Office's senior officer dealing with personnel matters) to make sure that he received the services of the officers that he wanted with him in V Corps. This infuriated Auchinleck, who responded with a formal complaint on August 15:

> I do not consider this is the proper manner in which this, or any other matter of this nature, should be handled. When orders are issued from these Headquarters, whether they come from the War Office or direct from these Headquarters, and you wish to make a protest, from whatever point of view, against these orders, I wish such protests to be made to these Headquarters and not to War Office officials over my head.[4]

As would be repeated again and again, Montgomery simply ignored the order and pushed ahead both with his reorganization of V Corps and with its tactical plans. In place of rigid beach defenses, Montgomery issued a new tactical doctrine that would see the beaches held by soldiers of the Home Guard, a part-time civilian force, while the two infantry divisions would train for counteroffensive operations. This was in direct opposition to Auchinleck's thinking, and it must have caused fresh friction between V Corps and Southern Command. It helped that Montgomery continued to receive Brooke's support and patronage, although the latter did remind him in a friendly letter on August 5 that he had gained a reputation for "annoying people" and that he was not to do "anything silly."[5]

Although Montgomery's behavior must have been extremely irritating to those around him, he was convinced that the country was involved in a life-or-death struggle, and that the Germans would only be defeated by a combination of sound training and preparation, the inculcation of an offensive spirit, and the provision of the right equipment. This would only be achieved by hard work, determination, and a willingness to make sacrifices for the greater good of the army. Above all, he insisted that the soldiers under his command should be "binged up"—"binge" being a favorite expression with no precise meaning much used by Montgomery to explain the creation and maintenance of high morale and fighting spirit. Training notes from a lecture given at Staff College in October 1940 provide insight into Montgomery's thinking during this period and make clear that "binge" was a crucial concept in making soldiers ready for battle:

> No good trying to fight a first class enemy unless the soldiers are absolutely on their toes.
> They must have a "stomach for the fight." They must have the light of battle in their eyes.
> They must look forward to a good fight.
> They must be full of "binge."
> Cannot be full of binge if you are not fit; must have that exhilaration that comes from physical well being; optomistic [sic] outlook on life; no good being pessimistic with a face like a piece of cheese.[6]

A study week was instituted for unit commanders between October 7 and 12, 1940, and emphasis was on Montgomery's message that the enemy could be beaten if every soldier was properly trained and prepared and knew exactly what was expected of them. Throughout this period Montgomery also made it his business to tour his corps area so that all soldiers, however junior, would recognize him. Other innovations included a major exercise at the beginning of December in which employed airborne troops, armored formations, and RAF light bombers flew in support of the advancing ground forces. The exercise, on Salisbury Plain, was designated as an imaginary area in the Middle East—which served them well, considering that would be their next theater of war.

By then the Battle of Britain had been fought and won in September 1940, and the German failure to win the upper hand in the air had forced Hitler to cancel his invasion plans. The German air offensive then turned to the bombing of cities in a bid to destroy the production of war materials (setting a precedent for the later bomber offensives used by both the Germans and the Allies). Meanwhile, Italy had joined the war on Germany's side, and in August Italian forces invaded British Somaliland and moved toward the border with Egypt. This moved the crucible of Britain's war against the Axis powers to the Middle East, where its 80,000-strong garrison was still under General Sir Archibald Wavell's command. To safeguard Egypt and the strategically vital Suez Canal, an offensive was mounted in December 1940 by the Western Desert Force, commanded by General Sir Richard O'Connor, who inflicted a decisive defeat on the larger Italian forces commanded by Marshal Rodolfo Graziani.

While the victory was a much-needed fillip to the British war effort—O'Connor's forces took Tripoli and defeated the Italian Tenth Army at Beda Fromm—it encouraged Hitler to send armored forces to North Africa under the command of General Erwin Rommel, whose task was not just to bolster the Italians but to invade Egypt and defeat the British. In March, Rommel counterattacked, pushing into Cyrenaica and winning back most of the territory captured by O'Connor, who had the misfortune to be taken prisoner. At this crucial juncture, Churchill pressured Wavell to send troops to Greece following the German invasion of Yugoslavia, but this only siphoned off troops from Egypt and led to a disastrous evacuation from Crete. Elsewhere, in the spring of 1941, British and Transjordanian forces effected regime change in Iraq to prevent Rashid Ali's government from siding with the Germans, a move that would have threatened the country's valuable oil supplies.

Desperate to see the Axis forces expelled from Libya, Churchill urged Wavell to go on the offensive, but two operations, Battleaxe and Brevity, failed, and in July 1941 Auchinleck took over command from Wavell. A fresh offensive, Crusader, enjoyed some success in the summer, but Rommel was able to regroup and secure Tripolitania, a coastal area in Libya. As his supply lines became more secure, thanks to German naval and air superiority in the eastern Mediterranean, Rommel launched a new attack in May 1942 to hit Allied positions in the area. The recently formed British Eighth Army, under the command of Lieutenant-General Neil Ritchie, was defeated at Gazala near the crucial port of Tobruk, which fell on June 21. Britain's fortunes were now at a nadir, and with Rommel's forces at Mersa Matruh, there was a danger that Egypt would be invaded. The Royal Navy's Mediterranean fleet was forced to leave its base at Alexandria; there was panic in Cairo; and morale in the Eighth Army slumped. A month later a hasty strike by Rommel was halted at the last realizable defensive position north of the Qattara Depression, close to the railway junction at El Alamein, where an initial action was fought with Axis force in July (also known as the First Battle of Alamein or First Alamein), but by then Auchinleck's leadership was in doubt—following the Gazala battle he had sacked Ritchie and taken over personal command of the Eighth Army.

In August 1942, Churchill traveled to Cairo with Brooke, now CIGS, to assess the situation. Their first impulse was to return Auchinleck to command of the Middle East and find a new commander for the Eighth Army, but during the discussions there was a clean sweep in the command structure. To begin with, both Brooke and Churchill were in agreement that Auchinleck would remain in overall command and that either Montgomery or Lieutenant-General W. H. E. Gott should take over the demoralized Eighth. Brooke favored Montgomery because he was "bounding with self-confidence and capable of instilling this confidence in the people under his command,"[7] but Churchill argued that Gott should be given the job. Known as "Strafer" Gott on account of his pugnacity, he had made a name for himself in the First World War having commanded the 7th Armoured Division at Gazala and First Alamein. A big man with an equally large personality, Gott was popular with the troops, but Brooke was concerned that he was "very tired" from the strain of fighting the desert war. However, Churchill admired Gott's offensive spirit, which was in direct contrast to Auchinleck's caution, and on August 6 the appointment was confirmed.

At the same time Churchill decided to split the Middle East command, with Auchinleck taking responsibility for the area east of the Suez Canal (Syria, Palestine, Transjordan, and Iraq) while a new Near East Command would be formed to the west (Egypt and Libya), under the leadership of Lieutenant-General Sir Harold Alexander, who had served with Montgomery during Dunkirk and had recently overseen the retreat of the British and Indian forces from Burma. According to Brooke, the decision caused him a good deal of personal unhappiness, not least because at one stage Churchill had offered him that same command. In his diary entry for August 6, Brooke admitted that the offer made his "heart race very fast," but he rejected it immediately, both because he knew little about desert warfare and because he believed that he could better contribute to the war effort by remaining close to the prime minister in his role as CIGS.

> Another point which I did not mention was that after working with the PM [prime minister] for close on 9 months I do feel at last that I can exercise a limited amount of control on some of his activities and that at last he is beginning to take my advice. I feel therefore that, tempting as the offer is by accepting it I should definitely be taking a course which would on the whole help the war least.[8]

Brooke's thinking was remarkably prescient. The next day Gott was flying back to Cairo from Eighth Army headquarters when his lumbering Bristol Bombay air transport was shot down by German fighters and he was killed. Command of the Eighth Army passed to Montgomery, working directly with Alexander, and beyond that, with Brooke and Churchill. This arrangement proved to be a winning combination and one that, from a British perspective, would affect the outcome of the war.

But this was not the first operational command offered to Montgomery in the summer of 1942. On August 7, he received a call from the War Office instructing him to take over command of a British task force in the planned Allied invasion of North Africa, which would be led by Lieutenant General Dwight D. Eisenhower, a relatively unknown U.S. general with a reputation for solid planning. Known as Operation Torch, the objective was to gain complete control of North Africa from the Atlantic to the Red Sea, starting with landings in Algeria and French Morocco before rolling up the Axis forces in Libya. At the same time, the Eighth Army would break out of Libya, defeat the Afrika Korps, and link up with the advancing Allied forces in Tunisia.

To understand the importance of the North African campaign, one must look at it in the context of the rest of the war, which by this time had spread to the rest of the world. By that time, following the infamous preemptive Japanese attack on Pearl Harbor in December 1941, the U.S. had entered the war on the Allies' side. The shock of the Japanese attack suggested that the war in the Pacific should have been given priority, but the strategic balance had slipped away from the Allies. Following the bombing of Pearl Harbor, Japan invaded Malaya and Singapore and quickly forced the British and Commonwealth forces' surrender, on February 15, 1942. The Philippines fell into Japanese hands three months later, by which time the Dutch East Indies had also been occupied. There was an obvious American desire for retribution, but against that urgent need U.S. war plans dictated a "Germany first" policy. This had been underscored at the first summit meeting between Churchill and U.S. President Franklin D. Roosevelt in Washington in December 1941, when the two leaders agreed that Germany would have to be defeated before they turned their attention to Japan. The conference also led to the establishment of the Combined Chiefs of Staff, composed of the British Chiefs of Staff and the American Joint Chiefs of Staff. Its first task was to create a timetable for the invasion of Europe and to lay plans for a direct attack on Germany by invading France and driving quickly across the enemy border.

Their thinking was that the opening of this second front would also take pressure off the Soviet Union, which had been invaded by German forces in the summer of 1941 and was fighting for its survival. To meet that need, Chief of Staff General George Marshall put forward plans for a cross-Channel invasion in autumn 1942. Marshall was bullish about the plan and believed that by attacking the heart of Germany the war would be shortened. Unless that happened, he argued, the Soviet Union would collapse and the war against Germany would last a further decade. However, the British were unhappy with the plan, which Brooke deemed reckless and likely to fail: "The prospects of success are small and dependent on a mass of unknowns, whilst the chances of disaster are great."[9] Churchill also opposed the idea and argued forcefully for a U.S. invasion of North Africa that would trap Axis forces in Libya and Egypt.

The clash between the rival plans put the coalition under immediate strain. Marshall thought that the North African campaign was a sideshow that would do nothing to dent the German war effort; only a direct attack on the German homeland would bring the war to an end. There were also fears on the U.S. side that the British plan was aimed at propping up its imperial holdings east of Suez. The stalemate was broken by Roosevelt, who made up his mind on July 25, 1942: the invasion of Europe was postponed; instead the immediate objective became North Africa.

❖

While these events had been unfolding, Montgomery had been making steady progress on the home front. In April 1941 he took over command of XII Corps, responsible for the defense of Kent. Once again he arrived at his new headquarters in whirlwind fashion, sacking senior officers and tearing up earlier plans to concentrate on defense of the beach areas. "A number of heads are being chopped off—the bag to date is 3 Brigadiers and 6 COs," he boasted to his GSO2, Lieutenant-Colonel Christopher "Kit" Dawnay on May 7. "The standard here was very low."[10]

Montgomery's tactics were not universally applauded—not least by those who had served with Auchinleck and remained loyal to him—but he was not content to simply cut out deadwood; he also wanted to encourage a new way of thinking and to rebuild team spirit. Following a large-scale exercise that summer, he concluded that the use of the division, a fighting formation of all arms, was the correct method for beating the German army.

In Montgomery's day, an infantry division consisted of three brigades, each made up of three infantry battalions and supported by divisional troops—reconnaissance, engineers, signals, antitank, light antiaircraft, and a machine-gun battalion. By contrast, an armored division was composed of an armored brigade of three of four armored regiments and an infantry brigade of three infantry battalions, plus relevant divisional troops. Once they had been properly trained and directed, Montgomery reckoned that these armored formations were the correct means for handling a large conscript army in battle and were preferable to the more usual brigade groups of mixed arms. Henceforth, in a new training paper he ordered the adoption of a different approach:

> Divisions must fight as divisions and under their own commanders with clear-cut tasks and definite objectives; only in this way will full value be got from the great fighting power of a Division; and only in this way will concentration of effort and co-operation of all arms be really effective.[11]

Montgomery also understood that the new doctrine would only be effective if the battle was fought according to a master plan he controlled and imposed on his subordinate commanders. In all his operational papers, he described this as "getting a firm grip," and it could only be achieved through a rigorous training regime with all units practicing continuously to enable them to efficiently carry out routine tasks such as battle drills. At its most basic, Montgomery's view was that getting a division battle-ready was all about teamwork, discipline, and leadership.

His reward had come at the end of 1941, when he was promoted to take over South-Eastern Command, which was made up of XII Corps and Canadian Corps. As he had done during earlier promotions, Montgomery concentrated on training, and it is possible that but for Auchinleck's failure in North Africa, he would have been remembered only for that aspect of soldiering. Instead, he found himself taking over command of the Eighth Army and ordered to drive the Germans out of Libya. As Montgomery recalled in his memoirs, this outcome was exactly what he wanted:

> Instead of carrying out an invasion of North Africa under a C-in-C whom I barely knew, I was to serve under a C-in-C I knew well [Alexander] and to take command of an Army which was at grips with a German and Italian Army under the command of Rommel—of whom I had heard great things. This was much more to my liking and I felt I could handle that business, and Rommel. So it was with a light heart and great confidence that I made preparations for going to Africa.[12]

However, by the time of Montgomery's appointment, British policy in North Africa could not be decided in isolation, and he would have to learn how to cooperate with the Americans and other Allies. For all concerned, it would be a steep learning curve.

CHAPTER FIVE

Desert Victory: The Battles of Alam Halfa and El Alamein

WHEN MONTGOMERY ARRIVED TO TAKE COMMAND OF THE EIGHTH Army in Cairo early in the morning of August 12, 1942, he was not impressed by what he found. Morale was low and there was a prevailing defeatism that percolated down from the top—orders had already been issued to retreat to the Nile delta in the event of a German breakthrough. That outcome seemed all too possible. To the east, in his positions between the Qattara Depression and the sea, Rommel's Afrika Korps was less than 60 miles away from Alexandria and at that stage still enjoyed large numbers—ten divisions to Montgomery's seven. From his intelligence sources, the German commander also knew of the panic that existed in Cairo, and he must have guessed that the fighting spirit of the Eighth Army would have been dented by the succession of defeats and the constant changes in leadership. But he also knew that he was running out of time. Allied airpower threatened his lines of communication—the ports of Benghazi and Tobruk were vulnerable to aerial bombardment—and every mile that his forces advanced increased the demand on his logistic support. At the same time, the U.S. entry into the war had given the Allies a decided advantage with the promised arrival of 300 badly needed Sherman tanks, due to arrive in September. By the end of August, German intelligence estimated that the Allies would soon possess 900 tanks, compared with the Afrika Korps' estimated 500. Everything pointed to the need to deliver a knockout blow before the Allied strength increased and Rommel's forces were outnumbered. His ultimate aim was to smash through the Allied defenses, seize the Suez Canal between Ismailia and Port Said, and take control of Egypt.

Montgomery knew that time was not on his side, either, and he set about his task with the same energy and commitment that had marked his earlier commands. Although Auchinleck preferred a less hurried handover, partly to mollify his wounded pride and partly because he argued that the Eighth Army was still reorganizing, Montgomery wanted to get to work straightaway. Not only was he desperate to impose his personality and his ideology on a demoralized army but he also wanted to quash the idea that there would be any withdrawal. Orders for retreat were torn up and he immediately set about planning to take the offensive back to Rommel's doorstep.

The swift pace of Montgomery's takeover was maintained the day after his arrival when he visited its tactical headquarters behind the Ruweisat Ridge. On the way, he was accompanied by his old friend Freddie de Guingand, who was acting as Brigadier General Staff (BGS) to the Eighth Army, and was therefore in a position to give Montgomery an accurate situation report. His assessment was downbeat and cautious, and he criticized such failings as a lack of cooperation between army and air force and the reliance on a rigid defensive system. Later, de Guingand admitted that he might have over-stressed the withdrawal plan, but by then Montgomery had clearly decided to seize the moment. Shortly after arriving at army headquarters, he issued a signal assuming immediate command of the Eighth Army—against Auchinleck's wishes—and summoning a conference of senior commanders that very evening. Even if he was not aware of it at the time, in taking those bold measures, Montgomery was creating the legend on which his reputation would be based—the new commander who came from nowhere to restore a demoralized army and turn it into a battle-winner. Montgomery's first order was brief and to the point: "Here we will stand and fight; there will be no further withdrawal. I have ordered that all plans and instructions dealing with a further withdrawal are to be burnt, and at once. We will stand and fight here. If we can't stay here alive, then let us stay here dead."[1]

The announcement had the desired effect, and those present at headquarters on the evening of August 13 would have echoed de Guingand's sentiments, recorded in his memoirs, that "We all went to bed that night with new hope in our hearts, and a great confidence in the future of our Army."[2]

Montgomery understood that he had much to do in a very short time, but already he had been aided by the arrival of intelligence summaries that showed Rommel was preparing to attack, possibly even by the end of the month. On this point the evidence was reasonably accurate, as Montgomery had access to tactical air reconnaissance as well as top-secret Ultra decrypts—intelligence gathered from signals enciphered on German Enigma and *Geheimschreiber* cipher machines. (The code was supposed to be unbreakable but had been decoded by British cryptographers early in the war.) These resources had been underemployed by Auchinleck, and Montgomery's use of them should be taken into account when evaluating his command of the Eighth Army. For example, on August 15, Rommel sent his plans for a proposed attack to Hitler in Berlin; less than 48 hours later, thanks to Ultra, a copy was in Montgomery's hands. First, the plans provided a timetable for the attack to begin at the end of the month, and second, they revealed that

Rommel would make a feint to the north toward the Ruweisat Ridge, but his main attack would come from the south, around the British left flank, before driving north toward the sea. For the embattled Eighth Army commanders, this was priceless information.

In the time that was left to him, little more than two weeks, Montgomery had to work hard to raise morale and to restore the confidence that had been lost at Gazala and earlier reverses. He also had to produce a plan to counter Rommel's forthcoming offensive. Over the years there has been much debate about its origins. Did Montgomery simply take a preexisting plan prepared under Auchinleck's leadership, or did he produce his own? Supporters of The Auk have argued that Montgomery adopted an earlier version and simply updated and refined it, but an examination of the relevant divisional war diaries shows that Montgomery's plan for the defensive battle was an original formula based largely on the information received from Ultra.[3] Based on this, he was able to argue that the newly arrived 44th Infantry Division be transferred from the delta to the Eighth Army, even though it was untried in battle. It would then be deployed on the Alam Halfa Ridge, which ran southwest-northeast across the battlefield for some 12 miles and provided a good defensive position against the expected assault from the south. To be fair, Auchinleck had identified it as such, but it was defended only by a weak force of two infantry battalions, whereas Montgomery saw the opportunity to use a fresh division that would otherwise have remained as garrison troops for the defense of the Suez Canal.

At the time, the Eighth Army was composed of XIII Corps (2nd New Zealand Division, 7th Armoured Division, 10th Armoured Division, and 44th Infantry Division) to the south and XXX Corps (9th Australian Division, 1st South African Division, and 5th Indian Division) to the north, between the Mediterranean and Ruweisat Ridge. Montgomery began inspecting his forces in the desert on August 14 and made an immediate impression. After he visited the New Zealand division, its commander, Lieutenant-General Bernard Freyberg, told his senior officers that there was now "a completely new outlook on the situation" and that it was his personal opinion that "it is a very good thing to get a completely new brain on the thing."[4] Although Montgomery told Freyberg that the next battle would be defensive, he added, "We shall be training on a long-term policy to resume the offensive as soon as it is possible." For men who had known only reverses and who had come to regard the enemy as invincible, these were encouraging words.

Montgomery's plan was to hold the main body of his armor in defensive positions with many of the tanks dug in, and to heavily reinforce his infantry positions with field and antitank artillery. The solidly mined area to the south would also provide a potent barrier, and the Desert Air Force's strike aircraft would attack the German armored columns once they had advanced into the open. Montgomery saw the battle as a trial of strength: the German and Italian forces would be drawn into ground of his choosing, and then their flanks would be attacked by the Eighth Army's armored brigades.

Rommel's approach was rather different. Knowing that time was against him, he placed his faith in the tactics that had served him so well earlier in the campaign. Following the feint to the north, six divisions would breach the southern defenses, then advance 20 miles eastward before heading north to the sea to cut off any British withdrawal. Once in the coastal plain, the panzer columns would race toward Cairo and Alexandria. Rommel assumed that the British would be drawn into a battle of maneuver in which they would be outclassed and outfought by his panzer commanders' superior tactics and leadership. That had happened in the past, and Rommel was confident that it would happen again. He knew that his opponents had a new general, but at that stage he knew very little about Montgomery or what kind of soldier he was. He would soon find out.

The attack began on the night of August 30 when three German and three Italian armored and motorized divisions moved rapidly into the southern gap before turning north, as anticipated, toward Alam Halfa. Almost immediately, Rommel's timetable was thrown into disarray. He had underestimated the size and potency of the southern minefield belt, and by dawn the panzer columns were still trying to find a way through them. All the while their progress was hindered by heavy artillery fire and ceaseless bombardment from the air as the Desert Air Force's bombers flew sortie after sortie. Still, the advance continued—though more slowly than Rommel had expected—and there was a further surprise when the Afrika Korps hooked north. As they approached the Alam Halfa Ridge, they discovered that it was more heavily defended than originally thought. The Eighth Army stood firm and made no attempt at engagement. When Rommel eventually ordered an assault on the western edge of the ridge, it was beaten off by the tanks of the 22nd Armoured Brigade on ground of their own choosing. During this phase of the fighting, the Germans lost Major-General Georg von Bismarck, the gifted commander of the 21st Panzer Division and, with casualties mounting, all momentum was lost.

Whereas Rommel viewed the Alam Halfa offensive as a last throw of the dice for his own offensive operations, Montgomery regarded it as a prelude—a defensive battle or holding operation before he could plan and launch an autumn offensive. Indeed, so sanguine was Montgomery about the outcome of the fighting that he retired to his bed before the Afrika Korps had launched its initial attack. By the morning of September 1, Rommel could see that there was no way forward. Faced with unmovable defenses and under constant aerial bombardment, Rommel made the decision to break off the battle the following day. Withdrawal began almost immediately, and although the Germans and Italians were able to save the majority of their tanks, they had suffered some casualties, with 3,000 either killed, wounded, or missing.

With the Afrika Korps in disarray and in retreat, Montgomery had the chance to counterattack and perhaps even destroy the opposition, but he did not take the bait. As history bore out, he was right to be cautious. Thanks to superior intelligence and Montgomery's disposition of his forces, the Battle of Alam Halfa had gone according to plan. The Afrika Korps had been halted and the Eighth Army had held its ground; now was not the time to squander that advantage.

(One such maneuver by the New Zealanders and a British brigade met with heavy casualties.)

Montgomery's failure to attempt a coup de grâce has been used by his critics to suggest that he neglected to act robustly when the opportunity arose, but that view misses the point. The outcome at Alam Halfa was a much-needed victory for the Eighth Army, but Montgomery had to conserve his forces for the offensive battle that would follow. In light of the Eighth Army's earlier reverses and its noticeable absence of aggressive capability, it was the right decision.

✦

The successful outcome put Montgomery under intense pressure from Churchill to move immediately against the enemy. The Eighth Army's commander's response was significant: Montgomery replied that if he was given until the third week of October—the time of a full moon—he could guarantee victory.[5] In making that bold assertion, he was either extremely foolhardy or remarkably sure of himself and his soldiers' abilities—perhaps both. In September, reinforcements started arriving in considerable numbers—the promised Sherman tanks, new six-pound antitank guns, and additional artillery pieces, as well as four new divisions—the 50th (Northumbrian) and 51st (Highland) Infantry Divisions and the 1st and 8th Armoured Divisions. By October, his army would consist of 195,000 men, 1,029 medium tanks, 1,451 anti-tank guns, and 500 artillery pieces. Against that Rommel possessed 104,000 soldiers (80,000 German), 496 medium tanks, 908 field guns, and 800 antitank guns. There was one other factor that came into play—the Eighth Army had solid lines of communication back into Egypt with steady supply and resupply, whereas the German and Italian supply lines across the Mediterranean were overextended and under constant attack by the Royal Air Force and the Royal Navy.

During the Battle of Alam Halfa, Rommel had fallen ill with high blood pressure and a stomach ailment, and on September 23, he was airlifted back to Germany for treatment. Before he left he ordered the Afrika Korps' minefields to be strengthened and for his weaker Italian units to be "corseted" by German formations. To counter the new depth and strength of the enemy's defenses, and to prevent a battle of maneuver that would give the advantage to Rommel's forces, Montgomery planned a set-piece battle with three distinct phases— the break-in, the dogfight, and the breakout, once the Axis defensive line had been breached. He decided to place the weight of the attack in the north, with the four infantry divisions of XXX Corps making the initial assault on a ten-mile front to allow two armored divisions of X Corps to pass beyond the bridgehead before engaging the German and Italian armor, playing the role of a *corps de chasse* (pursuit forces). At the same time, in an elaborate deception, an attack would be made from the south using XIII Corps, now under the command of Lieutenant-General Brian Horrocks, an educated soldier whose name would be associated with Montgomery for the rest of the war.

In typical Montgomery fashion, the master plan for the battle was relayed to the three corps commanders along with an admonition that there could be no changes. Inevitably, though, refinements were necessary. Throughout the Eighth Army there was considerable suspicion between armored and infantry commanders, each lacking confidence in the other, and as a result Montgomery decided to revise the plan to allow his armored forces to support the XXX Corps attack while the infantry protected the flanks from German antitank artillery. This would change the essential nature of the fighting into a formal battle, but given the timetable—Churchill was becoming increasingly anxious about delays— Montgomery was left with little option but to trim his plan. He explained his revised thinking in a memorandum written on October 6: "It was clear that I must so stage-manage the battle that my troops would be able to do what was demanded of them, and I must not be too ambitious in my demands."[6] However, by sacrificing the speed of a rapid armored thrust and substituting a slower combined assault, the fighting would take longer and become a battle of attrition. In that sense, it would also be a set-piece battle similar to the kind that had been fought in the latter stages of the First World War, with soldiers advancing under a heavy barrage and battalions leapfrogging forward to take their objectives.

In the run-up to the attack, Montgomery took the time and trouble to make sure that the men of the Eighth Army, especially the newly arrived reinforcements, knew exactly what was happening and what was expected of them. He also continued his policy of inspecting units right down to battalion level and talking to the men. Mostly such visits were a boost to morale, but there were occasional glitches: while spending time with the 154th Brigade in the newly arrived 51st (Highland) Division, he recognized the identity of the Regular 1st Black Watch, but he appeared to be dumbfounded when told that the 7th Black Watch, a Territorial battalion of the same regiment, came from the county of Fife in Scotland. (Like all British infantry regiments of the time, the Black Watch recruited from a specific area, in this case the Scottish counties of Angus, Fife, and Perthshire.) According to Brigadier H. W. Houldsworth, Black Watch officers "stood gaping with their mouths open" when Montgomery admitted that he did not know where Fife was as he had "never been to Scotland."[7]

On the eve of battle, the night of October 23, Montgomery issued a stirring personal message to every soldier in the Eighth Army, reminding them that their mission was to destroy Rommel's men, and that they were now ready to do it:

> The battle which is now about to begin will be one of the decisive battles of history. It will be the turning point of the war. The eyes of the whole world will be on us, watching which way the battle will swing. We can give them their answer at once, "It will swing our way."[8]

The opening rounds of the Battle of El Alamein were very encouraging, largely because Montgomery had achieved complete surprise. At 9:40 P.M., a huge artillery barrage opened up as hundreds of guns fired toward the enemy lines, and shortly after 10:00 P.M. the attacking force moved off, each infantry battalion guided by a navigation officer watching his compass and counting his paces to ensure accuracy. All the first objectives in the heavily defended Axis center were quickly taken, with the follow-up forces passing easily through the first wave, although some battalions pushed on too quickly and had to halt to wait for the artillery bombardment to pass. By dawn the vulnerable Miteiriya Ridge had been claimed by the British and Commonwealth forces. Later in the day, it also became clear that the Germans had lost Rommel's deputy, General Georg Stumme, who died of a heart attack while under fire in a forward position.

Inevitably, though, there were problems. In the north, the 51st (Highland) Division had encountered fierce resistance, which meant that the advance of the 1st Armoured Division had stalled, with several tanks being disabled in the minefields. Similar difficulties met the 10th Armoured Division, which meant that British tanks failed to engage their opponents by the deadline Montgomery had issued. Visibility was impaired by huge dust clouds created by the artillery and aerial bombardment, as well as by determined German antitank gunfire. One officer admitted the scene was "like a badly organized car park at an immense race meeting held in a dustbowl."[9] Further south there was similar confusion, and at dawn the Germans still held their positions. Casualties were also high: The 51st lost 1,000 men, while the New Zealanders fared little better, with 800 casualties (killed, wounded, or missing). To add to Montgomery's problems, Rommel returned from sick leave on October 25 and resumed command just as his forces repulsed a determined attack by the Australians in the northern sector between Kidney Ridge and the sea.

Realizing that further armored attacks would cause an unacceptable number of casualties, Montgomery decided to strengthen his positions for a fresh assault on October 28. There was an urgent need to stiffen the backbones of commanders in the field: Lieutenant-General Herbert Lumsden, commanding X Corps, was summoned to Montgomery's headquarters, where he was told "in no uncertain voice" that he must "drive" his divisional commanders. If they failed, warned Montgomery, they would be rapidly replaced. This had the desired effect, and following some sterling work by the 51st (Highland) Division, one of the brigades of the 1st Armoured Division broke out and captured its objective at Kidney Ridge, which was held by the 15th and 21st Panzer Divisions. Throughout this first period of the battle, Montgomery kept his nerve, and he wrote in his diary that his "application of 'ginger' had worked."[10]

By October 30, after five days of heavy fighting, the British attack had become a battle of attrition, and Montgomery responded accordingly by regrouping and preparing for a fresh offensive involving infantry and armor operating in tandem. The result was Operation Supercharge, which began on the night of November 1 with the 2nd New Zealand Division reinforced by two infantry and two armored brigades striking inland north of Kidney Ridge. At the same time, the Australians continued to press their increasingly fruitful attacks along the coast, while in the south, XIII Corps drove westward. Once a bridgehead had been established in the open desert, the path would be cleared for the 1st Armoured Division to break through and attack the Axis lines. This time the attack went well, and the supporting 9th Armoured Brigade was able to inflict heavy losses despite losing almost 70 percent of its own tank force.

In his directive to commanders, Montgomery insisted that every effort had to be made to secure victory, and that "risks must be accepted freely." By then, shortage of tanks and fuel meant that Rommel was in no position to counterattack as Montgomery's forces swept into the open ground beyond the crucial Rahman Track marking the German defensive line. After a hard, 12-day slog, the battle of attrition was over, and the pursuit phase was about to begin. Between them the Germans and Italians had lost up to 20,000 casualties, while 30,000 became prisoners of war. In contrast, casualties in the Eighth Army were 13,500.

In time, the names of Montgomery and El Alamein became synonymous. Eighth Army veterans basked in the fact that they had served under Monty when he won his great desert battle, and when he was elected to a peerage in 1946, he took as his title Field Marshal Viscount Montgomery of Alamein. Although it was neither the first nor the only victory over the Axis powers in North Africa—General Sir Richard O'Connor had achieved similar success two years earlier in the western desert—Alamein was a triumph that captured the popular imagination. After years of setbacks, the Germans and Italians had not just been beaten, but beaten decisively. With the loss of Singapore and Burma to the Japanese in the Pacific theater, it had not been a good year for the British war effort, so Montgomery's success at Alamein was a hugely significant victory. Plus, there was the added poignancy that it was to be the last time that British and Commonwealth forces would beat the Germans without the support of its larger ally, the United States.

From a strategic viewpoint, the victory had also helped to change the balance of the war. The result was comprehensive: Egypt was saved from the threat of invasion, and the Axis army was forced to remove itself from Cyrenaica, so weakened that any return was impossible. With Germany involved in an increasingly desperate war against the Soviet Union, Hitler was now faced with the reality of fighting a land war on two fronts.

For Montgomery, it was also a remarkable personal achievement. The battle was barely ten weeks after his arrival to take command of the Eighth Army, and he had used that time to good effect. He built up his forces until he had a superiority of two to one in manpower, five to two in armor and four to one in the air. By contrast, Rommel was restricted by insufficient fuel and a lack of reserves in personnel and material. However, it would be wrong to suggest that Montgomery won the battle simply through weight of numbers. His plan called for a battle of attrition in which his men would carefully build their striking forces before inexorably overcoming the Axis defenses in the north and then in the south. Only the depth and strength of the German minefield defenses prevented a speedier conclusion before the launch of Operation Supercharge. All told, it was an economical victory, well planned by Montgomery and robustly executed by his forces. No commander could have asked for more.

CHAPTER SIX

Pursuit into Tunisia

THE BRITISH VICTORY AT ALAMEIN WAS NOT THE END OF THE WAR, BUT as Churchill remarked at the time, in November 1942, it marked the beginning of the end. For the first time in the conflict, church bells were rung across the United Kingdom to celebrate the victory, which was not only decisive but desperately necessary for British morale. By midafternoon on November 4, the 7th and 10th Armoured Divisions had destroyed their Italian opponents and, unable to obey Hitler's order to stand fast, German general Erwin Rommel ordered his forces to begin a long retreat that would take them 2,000 miles back toward Tunisia. In the first hours of the operation, the New Zealanders almost cut them off at Fuka, but the onset of heavy rain made movement problematic, as did the roadblocks created by the advancing Eighth Army's transport and armored forces. Tank numbers and performance were also a problem for the British and Commonwealth forces. Although the Shermans had proven themselves in the recent fighting, their gas consumption (three miles per gallon) caused immense supply problems, and the obsolescent Grant and Crusader tanks had been no match for the German panzers.

Montgomery began pursuit of Rommel's forces during this phase of the operation, and later critics have had harsh words to say about his failure to complete the destruction of the retreating enemy. To some extent, it is true that he showed excessive caution in organizing this next stage of the operation to defeat Rommel, but this was an understandable reaction. His army had just fought and won a bruising battle—it needed to regroup and be resupplied and reinforced—and above all, it did not need to be exposed to risks. Rommel had shown himself to be a master of mobile warfare, and the retreating Afrika Korps was hardly a disorganized rabble. Once Rommel's forces had moved beyond Fuka—the one place where Eighth Army could have cut them off in the immediate aftermath of the battle—they were in the clear. A second chance at Mersa Matruh a few days later was also spurned by Montgomery, but by then Rommel was so anxious about the threat to his flanks that he chose to surrender Tobruk without a fight, abandoning key airfields at Derna and Benghazi. The German general was clearly attempting to force his opponents to outrun their supply lines before he counterattacked. Montgomery sensed this and wisely declined to split his forces; instead he decided to grind down the enemy by relentlessly pushing the opposition out of Libya and back into Tunisia.

It was not dramatic, but it made good sense, and the decision exemplified Montgomery's growing self-confidence. And in no other incident was Montgomery's showmanship better displayed than in the advance on the strategically important port of Tripoli, which fell at the end of January 1943. Its capture was the direct result of the earlier victory at Alamein, and Montgomery used it to reinforce the scale of Rommel's defeat and also to underline the Allies' growing strength. At dawn on January 23, the first British tanks entered the port, carrying infantrymen of the 1st Gordon Highlanders with their pipers playing the regimental quick march "Cock of the North," the moment captured by accompanying war correspondents. Two weeks later Montgomery capitalized on the publicity when Churchill visited Tripoli with Lieutenant-General Sir Harold Alexander and Lieutenant-General Sir Alan Brooke and entertained the party at the first British victory parade of the war. It was a full-blown ceremonial affair. Following a triumphal drive into the main square of Tripoli, the prime minister was treated to a march-past led by the pipes and drums of the 51st (Highland) Division. It was a scene that greatly moved those watching it, including Brooke, who recorded it in his diary.

> As I stood alongside of Winston watching the [Highland] Division march past, with the wild music of the pipes in my ears, I felt a large lump rise in my throat and a tear run down my face. I looked at Winston and saw several tears on his face, from which I knew he was being stirred inwardly by the same feelings that were causing such upheaval in me. It was partly due to the fact that the transformation of these men from their raw pink and white appearance in Ismailia to their bronzed war-hewn countenances provided a tangible and visible sign of the turn of the tide of war. The meaning of this momentous change was brought home to me more forcibly than it had been up to the present. For the first time I was beginning to live through the thrill of those first successes that were now rendering ultimate victory possible.[1]

Two other incidents revealed the difference in the fortunes of the opposing commanders. On November 11, Montgomery was knighted and promoted to full general; two weeks later Rommel was flown back to Berlin, where he was harangued by Hitler and ordered to hold the German positions at Mersa Brega in Tripolitania, regardless of cost and without any thought of surrender. Hitler's ire was perhaps understandable: while the interview with Rommel was taking place, he had begun receiving reports about the imminent collapse of General Friedrich Paulus's Sixth Army at Stalingrad, where the German strike into Russia had foundered and the invading forces were on the point of surrender. Viewed from that perspective, both defeats, Alamein and Stalingrad, represented massive setbacks to the Nazi cause.

Given the scale of Montgomery's victory and the dramatic reversal of Rommel's progress, it was not surprising that comparisons were made between the rival generals and their styles of leadership. These are instructive in considering Montgomery as a battlefield commander. Both men had served in the First World War, and both had emerged from the conflict with glowing reputations, but there the comparisons ended. As we have seen, Montgomery was a quintessential staff officer who placed great stock in careful planning, making the best use of scant resources, and the imposition of force. Rommel was rather different. No less dedicated than Montgomery in his approach to soldiering, he had come to the fore on the Italian front, where he displayed an instinctive feeling for handling mobile formations. For his services, he was awarded the Pour le Mérite, Germany's highest decoration for valor. Like Montgomery, he became an infantry trainer during the interwar years, and in 1937 he wrote the influential manual *Infantry Attacks,* a volume much admired by Hitler. In 1940, Rommel commanded the 7th Panzer Division during the invasion of France, where his élan in leading his men and his willingness to take risks reinforced his reputation as a dashing and forceful field commander.

With his belief in the necessity of attack, the use of surprise tactics, and the importance of personal leadership in battle, Rommel was the ideal commander for the African field, where the wide open spaces of the desert gave him full scope for taking an adventurous approach in a fast-running war of maneuver. Montgomery, on the other hand, was the exact opposite. He was careful not to join battle unless the odds were stacked in his favor; he was a master of organization and he carefully selected divisional commanders who would execute his plans without question. If the roles had been reversed after Alamein, Rommel would probably have pursued the defeated enemy relentlessly, whatever the risk to the safety of his forces. Whereas the German general favored improvisation and chance, Montgomery was a consolidator and a pragmatist, and these characteristics made him very careful with his men's lives.

In spite of the differences in their military doctrines, however, the two men had striking personal similarities. Both cared greatly about the well-being of the soldiers under their command and went to great lengths to ensure that they received the best equipment and training. Both were good communicators and made sure that their armies were always kept well informed about what was happening. Both men believed in maintaining their own physical fitness and were abstemious in their private lives. Publicity was important to both of them, and they were not averse to making themselves the center of it. Thanks to the efforts of the German propaganda machine, Rommel was hugely popular with the German public, and Montgomery had a reputation for grabbing the limelight with the accompanying British war correspondents. (By the time of Alamein, he had devised a trademark look that consisted of a black beret or bush hat adorned with various regiments' cap badges. Later he refined this to the black beret with the badge of the Royal Tank Regiment and his general's hat badge.) Other similarities included their impatience with subordinates and Allies, their insistence on high standards, and their ability to win the ear of their respective political leaders.

One other factor joined Rommel and Montgomery together. They were fighting in a landscape that had few comparisons with the other theaters of the Second World War, and both men seem to have been affected by its wild beauty. At first acquaintance the North African terrain was harsh, barren, and inhospitable; but it was also strangely compelling, a landscape that imprinted itself on the minds of the men who fought there. Soldier poet Hamish Henderson, an intelligence officer in the 51st (Highland) Division, described it in his elegy "End of a Campaign" as the "brutish desert . . . this landscape for half-wit stunted ill-will," while another soldier poet, Jocelyn Brooke, declared in "Landscape near Tobruk" that "this land was made for war."[2] In fact, few of the men who served there, writers or not, failed to be affected by the sheer size of the desert over which the two opposing armies fought, with its seemingly limitless horizons and few roads or tracks to break up the bare expanse of sand and scrub. Responding to the landscape's similarities with a Roman sporting arena, war correspondents on both sides tended to report the conflict using imagery that spoke of a courtly tournament involving valiant rivals rather than as a bloody battle involving tanks and high explosives.

In the final analysis of the Battle of El Alamein, one essential fact divides the two rival commanders: Montgomery was the ultimate victor, and there was considerable satisfaction in his own mind that he had been able, in some small measure, to avenge the disappointments of Dunkirk. He defeated Rommel at El Alamein and forced him to retreat to Tunisia, where the war in North Africa would finally be decided a few months later. By that stage, the Eighth Army was not fighting alone, and its pursuit of Rommel's forces was not happening in isolation. From this point onward, the operations to clear Axis forces from North Africa have to be seen in the context of the Allies' overall strategy.

On November 9, the U.S. Western Task Force had landed virtually unopposed at Casablanca, followed by further Allied landings at Oran and Algiers. However, the unwillingness of some Vichy French leaders to negotiate with the Allies proved a stumbling block. This gave the Germans and the Italians time to reinforce Tunisia and to create the Fifth Panzer Army under the command of Colonel-General Hans-Jürgen von Arnim, a veteran of the Russian front. By the end of 1942, he had 100,000 troops under his command, most of them experienced in battle conditions, and he also enjoyed the luxury of air superiority with Luftwaffe fighters and bombers flying at will from bases in Sicily and Tunisia. Even the weather conspired to help the panzer army—an Allied offensive mounted before Christmas quickly became bogged down in heavy winter rain, which made movement all but impossible. Suddenly, a quick Allied victory in Tunisia seemed only a remote possibility. Following Montgomery's success at El Alamein, Eisenhower had been made to look slow, overcautious, and inexperienced, and there were serious cracks in the Allied command structure. There were also failures in field command. The senior British commander of the First British Army (consisting of the British V Corps, French XIX

Corps, and U.S. II Corps), Lieutenant-General Kenneth Anderson, hesitated to press an attack on Tunis, while the commander of U.S. II Corps, Major General Lloyd Fredendall, showed that he was unfit to command when his forces suffered ignominious defeats at the hands of Rommel at Sidi-Bou-Zid and the Kasserine Pass in February 1943. He was replaced by Lieutenant General George S. Patton.

Following a conference of Allied leaders in Casablanca in January of that year (codenamed Symbol), Harold Alexander had been ordered to complete the Tunisian operations by the end of April so that planning could begin for the invasion of Sicily as a precursor to invading Italy. He was under intense pressure to keep to the timetable, and in February took over command of the 18th Army Group, responsible for all operations in North Africa. After the relatively easy victory at the Kasserine Pass, Rommel prepared to attack the Eighth Army at Medenine while his Colonel-General von Arnim made a number of diversionary attacks to the north. During the subsequent fighting, Montgomery's forces held firm, and in the aftermath there was some much-needed good fortune when Rommel once again fell ill and was replaced by von Armin as commander in chief of the German forces. At the same time, the German-Italian Panzer Army was renamed the First Italian Army and placed under the operational command of Marshal Giovanni Messe, an experienced soldier. By the beginning of March, Messe had taken up a defensive position along the Mareth Line, which ran 22 miles inland from the Mediterranean to the Matmata Hills in southern Tunisia.

While this was happening, von Arnim made preparations to defend Tunis with forces that were not only outnumbered but were now lacking vital supplies and reinforcement, thanks to the Allied naval blockade in the Mediterranean. The Allied plan was to use Anderson's First Army to push eastward on a broad front between the Mediterranean and the mountains of the Eastern Dorsal, while Montgomery's Eighth Army attacked the Mareth Line from the south. If the assault succeeded, Messe's army would be driven north along the coastal plain to Tunis, where they and von Arnim's forces would be crushed by the advancing Allies. The trouble was that Montgomery had a poor opinion of the First Army and was particularly exercised by the performance of the U.S. forces during the heavy defeat at Kasserine, which had allowed Rommel to split the Allied line in Tunisia and passed the advantage back to the Axis forces. A subsequent setback at Gafsa a few days later did nothing to reverse Montgomery's increasingly hostile opinion of the First Army's capacities. Unfortunately, it also added to a growing perception that the U.S. forces in particular were still green and had not yet been subjected to the stresses and strains of combat. This thinking would have serious implications for the operations that lay in the months ahead.

Montgomery's riposte to the new enemy alignment was a fresh offensive, Operation Pugilist, which would allow the Eighth Army to break through the enemy lines at Mareth and capture the coastal town of Gaba before moving northeast toward Sfax. Once again, the operation's success was predicated on the need to build up reserves and then to use overwhelming force in the assault phase. Once again, too, Montgomery showed that he would not take any chances against an experienced and battle-hardened enemy. However, Eighth Army confidence was high. Having fought off Rommel during a short and sharp encounter at Medenine on March 6, Montgomery believed that a successful onslaught could even take his forces as far as the southern approaches to Tunis. "My soldiers are full of beans," he told Brooke, "and we will take a lot of stopping." Privately, Montgomery even thought that the advance would prove unstoppable and that his men would be able to race rapidly north "in one bound."[3]

He was right in one respect—in that the final advance to Tunis only took three weeks—but he was wrong in thinking that the German defenses along the Mareth Line would crumble quickly in the face of the initial attack on March 20. The plan was to establish a bridgehead at Wadi Zigzaou between Mareth and the Metmata Hills while Freyberg's New Zealand Division launched a wide-flanking attack to the south, feinting west before sweeping north and east toward Gabes. Before the attack began, the artillery opened fire with the largest barrage since El Alamein, but before long the infantry divisions of XXX Corps were in trouble. Attacking along a narrow front, men and vehicles got bogged down in the sands of the Wadi, and the break-in foundered. To sustain momentum, Montgomery ordered an armored brigade to reinforce the narrow bridgehead, but by then the Germans had regrouped, and the attack continued to stall. By dawn on March 22, the New Zealanders had been blocked at the Tebaga Gap, and XXX Corps was making no progress. In some places infantrymen were involved in close-quarter fighting, and in one ferocious action, an entire tank regiment was more or less wiped out after the Germans counterattacked with the powerful new Tiger tanks equipped with 88-millimeter guns. There was also a fair degree of confusion among divisional commanders regarding events in other parts of the battlefield—Major-General Douglas Wimberley, commanding the 51st (Highland) Division, noted in his war diary "all this time it was very difficult to get any sort of picture of what was really happening."[4]

Throughout this difficult and anxious night, when it seemed that Eighth Army might have to withdraw from the bridgehead, Montgomery was asleep in his caravan and had to be awakened to deal with the crisis. He faced a worrying situation. Ever since assuming command in North Africa, he had made it clear that there were to be no more withdrawals; but at the same time, a stand at Wadi Zigzaou could create unacceptable casualties. (One formation, the 151st Infantry Brigade, had already lost 600 men.) Defeat was staring him in the face, and he must have realized that any setback on the Mareth Line would wipe out all the gains made at Alamein and set back the timetable for the invasion of Sicily. Faced by the possibility of calamity, Montgomery reacted calmly and logically and in so doing he restored order and self-confidence in those under him. At this crucial moment, when the battle could easily have been lost, strong leadership was required—and that was exactly what Montgomery provided.

At senior officers' conference the following morning, March 23, Montgomery decided to call off the frontal assault and to concentrate the weight of his attack on the left hook using the 1st Armoured Division and X Corps. At the same time, he sent a signal to Alexander requesting Patton's U.S. II Corps to advance toward Gabes while the Desert Air Force prepared to back up the fresh armored assault toward the Tebaga Gap. Led by the New Zealand infantry, the renewed attack began on March 26, and within two days the Corps occupied a new line from El Hamma to Gabes, forcing Messe's forces to withdraw. Patton had also moved forward to El Guettar, but his attack slowed down when the U.S. 1st Armored Division ran out of steam; as a result, U.S. II Corps was unable to break out of the Eastern Dorsal. Instead of being pinioned between two forces, Messe was able to withdraw his army toward Wadi Akarit, but by then the immediate danger facing Eighth Army was over. By refusing to panic and by pulling out of a potentially disastrous stalemate on the Mareth Line, Montgomery regained the upper hand, and on March 29, Alexander sent a congratulatory signal stating that El Hamma (as the engagement became known) had been "a decisive success."[5]

From the El Hamma-Gabes line, Montgomery pushed on to the next obstacle at Wadi Akarit, which was attacked on April 6. Although the Germans and Italians occupied a strong defensive position, they were taken by surprise when they came under intensive attack by the infantry of the 51st (Highland) Division and 4th (Indian) Division and were in full retreat within a matter of hours. Unlike the fighting on the Mareth Line, this was an attack of great strength, and only a failure to pursue the retreating enemy allowed Messe's forces to withdraw north as far as Enfidaville. However, it was also the beginning of the end of the campaign, as first contact had been made between the First and Eighth Armies. There was a regrouping of formations to reinforce the First Army, with the Eighth Army losing two armored and one infantry division, as well as much of the medium artillery and other divisional troops, for the final attack on Tunis, which fell on May 13.

◆

This was probably the high-water mark of the Eighth Army's war in North Africa. After three years of hard fighting, in which they had frequently been on the defensive, British troops were now in ascendance, and the men under Montgomery's command had undoubtedly developed a good conceit of themselves and their abilities. Unfortunately for Allied solidarity, so too had the general commanding them. Following the defeat of U.S. forces at Kasserine and the failure to act decisively at El Guettar, Montgomery had come to the conclusion that U.S. forces were not battle-worthy, and he tended to agree with Alexander's assessment that it was not commanders like Patton who gave cause for concern, but the quality of the soldiers under them: "The trouble as I have said is with the troops on the ground who are mentally and physically rather soft and very green," wrote Alexander on March 29. "It's the old story again—lack of proper training, allied to no experience of war—and too high a standard of living."[6] This adverse view of the U.S. war effort also extended to Eisenhower, who visited Eighth Army headquarters before the Battle of Wadi Akarit. After, Montgomery confided his impressions to Brooke:

> The American contribution to the party up to date has been very disappointing. Eisenhower came and stayed with me on 31 March. He is a nice chap. I should say he is probably quite good on the political side. But I can say, quite definitely, that he knows nothing about how to make war or fight battles; he should be kept right away from all that business if we want to win this war.[7]

This judgment was unfair, as Montgomery had no experience with the U.S. forces; and while he was correct to praise Eisenhower's political astuteness, he failed to understand the huge pressure under which he had been operating in this first coalition campaign. That being said, Eisenhower gave as good as he got, sending a "secret and confidential" memo to Marshall on April 6 in which he described Montgomery as "very conceited" and incapable of winning a battle "until he is absolutely certain of success—in other words, until he has concentrated enough resources so that anybody could practically guarantee the outcome."[8]

In both men's assessments there is an element of truth. Montgomery could be smug and arrogant, and at that stage of the conflict Eisenhower was still a novice with much to learn. It was also true that the U.S. forces had not performed to the best of their abilities, but to their credit, their experiences in Tunisia made them quick learners, and they could only improve. Not least, they had won the grudging respect of their opponents: even Rommel was forced to admit that the Americans had learned from their mistakes, had shown flexibility, and had made good use of their modern equipment:

> In Tunisia the Americans had to pay a stiff price for their experience, but it brought rich dividends. Even at that time, the American generals showed themselves to be very advanced in the tactical handling of their forces.... The Americans, it is fair to say, profited more than the British from their experience in warfare, thus confirming the axiom that education is easier than re-education.[9]

The rivalry between the British and U.S. forces would eventually give way to grudging respect, but it remained a factor until the end of the war, and the relationship between Montgomery and Eisenhower would never be easy. For that reason one can only deplore an embarrassing incident that occurred in the wake of Eighth Army's rapid advance into Tunisia.

During a visit to Montgomery's headquarters, Eisenhower's chief of staff, General Walter Bedell Smith, accepted a bet from Montgomery that the British general would receive a U.S. B-17 Flying Fortress bomber complete with crew if he captured Sfax by April 15.

Throughout the war, Montgomery was fond of betting small sums of money on practically anything, and when the wager was entered in the headquarters' betting book, Smith probably thought nothing of it. However, when Sfax fell on April 10, a delighted Montgomery sent a "most immediate" signal to Eisenhower recalling the wager and demanding the immediate dispatch of the promised Flying Fortress for use as his personal aircraft. When no reply was forthcoming, he kept up the pressure until the aircraft was delivered to him.

Later, Montgomery insisted that the Flying Fortress had been given willingly and that the incident had caused no friction with either Eisenhower or Smith, but Brooke was less sanguine. When the matter came to his attention, he castigated Montgomery for his "crass stupidity" for an action that "laid the foundations of distrust and dislike which remained with Eisenhower during the rest of the war."[10] The best that can be said about the incident is that Montgomery genuinely believed that it was all a bit of a joke in which Eisenhower was happy to participate, but in view of later friction between the two commanders, it was an unfortunate start to their working relationship.

CHAPTER SEVEN

Operation Husky

FOLLOWING THE VICTORY IN NORTH AFRICA, THE NEXT STAGE OF THE war against the Axis forces involved the capture of Sicily as a precursor to an invasion of Italy, a move the Allies hoped would lead to the final securing of the Mediterranean with its vital maritime routes. However, even before the operation began, its planning was dogged by disagreements and acrimony. U.S. General George Marshall still wanted to press ahead plans for the invasion of France and northern Europe. He favored a hard hit to Nazi Germany as the only way to win the war and did not want U.S. forces tied down in interminable operations in the Mediterranean, which he regarded as a strategic backwater. At the same time, Churchill remained preoccupied with attacking what he called on numerous occasions the "soft underbelly of Europe," both as a means of engaging the Germans and knocking Italy out of the war. As described by his biographer Martin Gilbert, Churchill's aim was "to persuade the

Americans to follow up the imminent conquest of Sicily by the invasion of Italy at least as far as Rome, and then to assist the Yugoslav, Greek and Albanian partisans in the liberation of the Balkans, by air support, arms and coastal landings by small Commando units."[1] At the Casablanca conference in 1943, there had been a marked divergence of opinion over the choice of Sicily (code-named "Husky"); Sardinia or Corsica was preferred by some planners. Then, of course, there was the slow rate of progress in Tunisia: senior commanders earmarked for Operation Husky, including Montgomery and U.S. General George Patton, were tied up in the fighting there until its final stages. As Montgomery protested to Harold Alexander on April 4, the day before the assault on Wadi Akarit: "It is very difficult to fight one campaign and at the same time to plan another in detail. But if we can get the general layout of HUSKY right other people can get on with the detail."[2] Later, as the planning became more confused and less focused, Montgomery would complain that the operation was "a dog's breakfast" (a favorite expression to describe his disgust at muddled thinking) that broke every basic rule about fighting the Axis. He felt it was doomed due to a failing that he always characterized as "a lack of grip." It is against that background of uncertain aims and Allied bickering that the British and U.S. roles in the Sicilian campaign should be seen.

In the middle of April 1943, having been relieved of command of U.S. II Corps, Patton returned to Casablanca to prepare the U.S. I Armored Corps for the forthcoming invasion. Ostensibly, as one of the invasion commanders—Montgomery, in charge of the British Eighth Army, was the other—Patton should have played a leading role in the planning of Husky, but so bitter were the British interservice rivalries and the lack of cohesion that he was left out in the cold. Command of the operation had been given to Alexander (Fifteenth Army Group), under U.S. Lieutenant General Dwight D. Eisenhower's nominal direction, but apart from Patton, all the senior commanders were British. The Allied naval forces were commanded by Admiral Sir Andrew Cunningham of the Royal Navy, while the air forces were under the direction of Air Chief Marshal Sir Arthur Tedder of the Royal Air Force. Not only were the Americans effectively frozen out of the senior command structure, but existing rivalries among the British commanders meant that the invasion plan was prolix in approach and protracted in development and execution.

In the original outline, Alexander's staff put forward proposals for an amphibious assault along the Sicilian coastline, with the attacking forces coming from the western and eastern Mediterranean. While this had the advantage of surprise—if it could be mounted quickly against what was then a weakly defended island—the operation carried with it the danger of being piecemeal and lacking in concentration. Another drawback was the failure to integrate the air element into the planning. Tedder had insisted that his squadrons would require the land forces to seize airfields for his strike aircraft so that air cover could be provided throughout the operation. The ensuing round of discussions were marred by undignified arguing and prevarication, and the deadlock was only broken by the intervention of Montgomery, who was quite capable of defending his corner and whose reputation as a battlefield commander had been greatly enhanced by his victories in North Africa. He refused to carry out the original plan, which obliged him to produce an alternative solution. Although Montgomery had given his tentative blessing to the first set of plans, he now opposed them vehemently, leaving Alexander with the option of either firing him for his presumption or agreeing with what he had to say.

On May 2, the revised plans were accepted. Montgomery's proposal called for an invasion by the Eighth Army, launched between Syracuse and the Pachino peninsula on the island's southeastern coast, while Patton's I and II Armored Corps, shortly to be renamed the U.S. Seventh Army (to give him parity with Montgomery) would land on a 40-mile front along the southern coast between Gela and Scoglitti and Licata on the left flank. There would also be an airborne assault carried out by the U.S. 82nd Airborne Division and the British 1st Airborne Division to attack targets in the inland area and to secure the landing grounds. For this first major combined land, sea, and air operation against a European target, overwhelming force would be used: 478,000 troops (250,000 British; 228,000 American) and 4,000 Allied aircraft. The landing forces would consist of an Eastern Naval Task Force under British command (795 warships and 715 landing craft) and a Western Naval Task Force under U.S. command (580 warships and 1,124 landing craft). Once ashore, Montgomery planned to create a bridgehead to secure the ports of Syracuse and Licata before moving rapidly north to Messina, while Patton's forces guarded his left flank.

On May 4, Alexander wrote a letter to Eisenhower at his headquarters in Algiers outlining the new plan, which seemed to suggest that the overall commander on the ground would be Montgomery. This was, in fact, his express request:

> As a result of acceptance by all concerned of present plan, land operations by British and American Task Forces really become one operation. Each will be dependent on the other for direct support in the battle and their administrative needs. As time is pressing, I am convinced that the co-ordination, direction and control both tactically and administratively, must be undertaken by one commander and a joint staff.[3]

Alexander did not say that the one commander would be Montgomery. He did not have to; Eisenhower would have had little difficulty guessing, and he noted Alexander's comment that Montgomery had offered to be as helpful as possible "in overcoming the problems facing the American Task Force." As placing U.S. troops under British command would be deleterious to American public opinion, a further compromise was introduced to allow the British and U.S. generals to retain their independent commands after landing. The arrangement seemed to suit Patton, who was anxious to get back into battle. Three days later he wrote in his diary: "The new set up is better in many ways than the old.... Monty is a forceful selfish man, but still a man, I think he is a far better leader than Alexander."[4]

After the operational plan had been set, the invasion of Sicily was one of the many topics discussed at the Trident Conference held in Washington between May 11 and 25. Described as the most ill-tempered of all the wartime Allied meetings, Trident pitted British against U.S. interests, with both sides at loggerheads over future Allied strategy. At the first meeting of the Joint Chiefs of Staffs, Marshall said that he regarded the North African strategy "with a jaundiced eye" and reiterated his preference for "cross-Channel operations for the liberation of France and advance on Germany." Brooke was equally adamant that the Allies should exploit the victory in Tunis with the invasion of Sicily, followed by the elimination of Italy from the war. Although the British Chief of the Imperial General Staff acknowledged that the "Americans wanted to close down all operations in Med after capture of Sicily," a compromise was reached when the British agreed to take part in an Allied cross-Channel invasion the following year, the price being U.S. approval for further operations in Italy (although the final report made no mention of this commitment).[5]

The date of the Sicilian invasion was fixed for July 10, but the delay provided time for the Germans and Italians to reinforce the island. During the campaign in North Africa, Sicily was defended by General Alfredo Guzzoni's Sixth Army, which consisted of four field divisions and six badly equipped and undermanned coastal defense divisions. By the end of June, these had been supplemented by a German panzer division and a new division formed out of reinforcements bound for North Africa (the 15th Panzergrenadier). Later these would be bolstered by the German 1st Parachute Division and the 29th Panzergrenadier Division, both drawn from France. Guzzoni's plan was to allow the weaker coastal divisions to bear the brunt of the Allied assault while the remaining forces, including the Germans, regrouped for a counterattack to drive the enemy back to the beaches.

Although Montgomery had taken into consideration the growing strength of the Axis defenses, Ultra intelligence intercepts suggested that the Italian soldiers' morale was low, and there was good reason to believe that the landings would be virtually unopposed. On the day itself, bad weather conditions created problems, but by late afternoon on July 10, Montgomery's two corps (XIII and XXX) were safely ashore between Pozallo and Syracuse to the east, while Patton's forces had taken the beaches between Cape Scaramia and Licata to the southwest. Within a few hours, all Allied divisions were ashore and the port of Syracuse had been captured intact. Forty-eight hours later, Montgomery believed that the route to Messina was open and that Axis resistance would crumble as his forces advanced up the eastern littoral:

> The battle in SICILY is a battle of key points. The countryside is mountainous and the roads poor. The few big main roads are two-way and very good; these run North-South and East-West, and once you hold the main centres of inter-communication you can put a stranglehold on enemy movement and so dominate the operations. As we drive forward on the main axes so the enemy tries to escape down the side lateral roads; but they cannot actually get away, and are then rounded up in large numbers. On the right flank—the sea flank—the Navy moves along keeping touch with the land battle and bombards effectively towns and villages where resistance is being offered. Fought in this way the battle is simple and the enemy is being forced back by our relentless pressure. On my left the American 7th Army is not making very great progress at present; but as my left [XXX] Corps pushes forward that will tend to loosen resistance in front of the Americans.[6]

Had Montgomery confined his thinking to his diary, all might have been well, but he sent a similar signal to Alexander, broadly hinting that he was in pole position to take Messina and that the Americans should play a supporting role by covering his left flank. Montgomery had been lulled into thinking that the lack of immediate resistance meant that the battle was as good as won. He was wrong, and by planting in Alexander's mind the idea that he should lead the advance on

Messina, with the U.S. forces playing a subsidiary role, Montgomery had created the conditions for an open clash with Patton. Their rivalry was to be one of the hallmarks of the Sicilian campaign.

The weather, too, continued to be a factor. Following the landings, it deteriorated with fresh summer storms followed by hot, stifling temperatures, hampering a rapid advance. Then there was an unforced disaster involving the Allied airborne assault's air landing and parachute troops. On the night of the operation, the winds were up to 35 miles per hour, and many of the British gliders had been shot down by Allied fire or landed in the sea before they reached their targets. Of the total force of 144 gliders, only 54 landed in Sicily; and of that number, only a dozen reached the correct landing grounds. The paratroopers of the U.S. 82nd Airborne Division fared equally badly. Either they were dropped in the wrong place or failed to reach the dropping zone over the southern part of the island after their transports got lost or were fired on by Allied shipping—a direct result of the lack of inter-service planning.

It was at this crucial early stage that Operation Husky began to unravel. As understood by Alexander, the British Eighth Army would provide the sword thrust toward Messina while the U.S. Seventh Army would act as its shield to block any counterattack. While this might have worked in theory, it made little sense in practice. First, there was no plan to allow Patton and Montgomery to work in concert. Second, the division of effort took no account of the island's difficult topography. Third, Alexander did not impose his will on the battle, a failure that allowed two headstrong army commanders on the ground to act independently of one another. Last, Alexander did not grasp that the Americans who fought in Sicily were very different from the tyros who had given such a poor performance in North Africa.

Unusually for him, Patton did not question how Montgomery had taken control of the operation, and he agreed to the plan without challenging it. The most salient explanation was the sudden deterioration in his relationship with Eisenhower, who had blamed him, unfairly, for the friendly-fire incidents involving the airborne forces. With the fear of dismissal hanging over him, Patton was in no position to question an unwise demand from Montgomery to hand Highway 124 over to British control, the main highway leading north. At the time, it was partially controlled by the U.S. 45th Division, which was making good headway in its advance from Vizzini toward Caltagirone. Now they were forced to make way for Montgomery's forces. Not only did the request deepen American mistrust of British motives, it was a tactical mistake, as the removal of the U.S. forces prevented Lieutenant-General Omar N. Bradley from deploying U.S II Corps northward to cut the island in half. If Bradley had been allowed to push ahead, there was every chance that the German 15th Panzergrenadier Division would have been cut off from its escape route toward Messina. It was a move that was later deprecated by the British corps commander, Lieutenant-General Sir Oliver Leese:

> I often think now that it was an unfortunate decision not to hand it [Highway 124] to the Americans. Unknown at any rate to XXX Corps, they were making much quicker progress than ourselves, largely owing, I believe, to the fact that their vehicles all had four-wheel drive. They were therefore far better equipped to compete quickly with the endless deviations with which we were confronted, as a result of the destruction of every bridge by the Germans. We were still inclined to remember the slow American progress in the early stages in Tunisia, and I for one certainly did not realise the immense development in experience and technique which they had made in the last weeks of the North African campaign. I have a feeling now that if they could have driven straight up this road, we might have had a chance to end this frustrating campaign sooner.[7]

That observation was written with the benefit of hindsight, but as expressed by Nigel Hamilton, Montgomery's official biographer, Leese's opinion is noteworthy because it provides an insight into the problem facing the ground commanders. Tactical sense suggested that the decision to hand over the highway played into the defenders' hands by allowing them to regroup, but in the absence of any overall plan, Patton was forced to concede to the British request. As it was, the Eighth Army did not require use of the entire highway, but this was not explained to the Americans, who thought that their role was being usurped at a time of progress.

The boundary-line incident did nothing to create any goodwill between the two armies, but events were about to change. Far from being able to push quickly toward Messina, Montgomery's forces became bogged down in the breakout from Syracuse. It was unpromising territory, but it had to be secured if the advance was to maintain its timetable. Unfortunately, it was also a countryside made for defense. Towering over the plain was the smoking hulk of Mount Etna, which the enemy used to good effect to observe the Allied movements. The Germans also enjoyed air superiority, and although some airfields had been captured by the Allies, it took time for aircraft to arrive and mount sorties against the enemy. Topographical considerations prevented Montgomery from utilizing his armor and artillery, and the lack of a decent road system meant that the infantry had to return to slogging by foot. The presence of civilians in the battlefield areas was also a hindrance. In short, after the freedom of movement enjoyed in North Africa, the Eighth Army found itself hemmed in, and the Plain of Catania proved to be a difficult hurdle. On the night of July 13, an airborne operation by the 1st Parachute Brigade failed to take the vital bridges at Primasole, and as a result, Catania remained in enemy hands.

Compounding the problems for the British, Leese's XXX Corps ran into fierce opposition as it moved over the mountainous terrain toward Enna and Leonforte, while XIII Corps was halted in its tracks on the road to Catania. It was almost as if the Axis defenders knew Montgomery's plan, and their unexpected resistance forced him to hook inland around the obstacle of Mount Etna. The operation was not an immediate success: the Canadian 1st Division clashed with the German 15th Panzer Division and was forced to wait for reinforcement from the 51st (Highland) Division. This delay gave Patton the chance to do something different while his British allies were distracted by their sudden reversals. Taking the view that there was enough room on the island for both armies to operate, Patton approached Alexander on July 17 with a proposal to move westward to capture the port of Agrigento. Permission was granted, providing that the Americans did not provoke a major battle that would threaten Montgomery's flank. Patton agreed, in the interests of maintaining Allied solidarity, but the unexpected decision provided him with the opportunity for greater U.S. involvement in the battle. While the U.S. 3rd Division attacked Agrigento, the rest of U.S. II Corps moved quickly north toward the coast to take the ports of Termini Imerese and Palermo.

On paper, the operation to seize the Sicilian capital served no useful purpose, but it did impress Alexander, by demonstrating that the U.S. Seventh Army was now a fighting force worthy of his attention. Two days later, the U.S. 45th Division reached the northern coast; Sicily was cut in half, and Patton was well placed to consider the next target—the prize, Messina. On July 25, Montgomery asked him to fly to Syracuse to decide the next phase of the operation. It was the first time that the two leaders had conferred since Husky began, and the outcome of their deliberations would be decisive in confirming Patton's growing reputation as a battlefield soldier.

That conference and the one that followed three days later also gave rise to the much-repeated story that Patton and Montgomery were involved in a heated rivalry to be the first general to take Messina. It made for good drama at the time and has been regularly cited, mainly in U.S. accounts, but it is in fact complete nonsense. By that stage in the battle, Montgomery realized that the Eighth Army could not take Messina single-handedly, and he therefore gave Patton permission take control of both the major roads north of Etna. He noted the revised thinking in his diary on July 28: "On my left I urged that 7 American Army [sic] should develop with two strong thrusts. (a) With two Divisions on the axis NICOSIA-TROINA-RANDAZZO. With two Divisions on the axis of the North coast road to MESSINA. This was all agreed."[8]

For the next stage of the war, Montgomery's thinking was sound. Ahead lay the invasion of Italy, and he was not prepared to sacrifice his men's lives when the U.S. forces were equally well placed to attack Messina. Two days before meeting Patton, he informed Alexander of his intentions: "Consider that whole operation of extension of war on to mainland [Italy] must now be handled by Eighth Army as once SICILY is cleared of enemy a great deal of my resources can be put on to mainland."[9] Under those circumstances, it made better sense to rest his own men and to pass the main thrust of the battle on to the U.S. Seventh Army. So Messina was handed on a plate to an astonished Patton, who was forced to realign his forces for an attack along the northern coast of Sicily as the enemy forces retreated to safety over the straits to southern Italy.

Although Patton did not know it, the race for Messina was over almost before it had begun. The Germans were not prepared to hand it over without a struggle, but steps had already been taken to surrender Sicily. The commander-in-chief of the Axis forces, Field Marshal Albert Kesselring, was determined not to repeat the defeat in Tunisia, and shortly after the Allied landings, he decided to pull out his forces to make them available for the defense of Italy. His plan was simple but effective. General Hans-Valentin Hube, now commander of the Axis ground forces, was ordered to form a strong defensive perimeter around Messina and to prepare for an evacuation in the second week of August. Every Luftwaffe aircraft within range was put into the air to provide cover for the dangerous crossing, while large antiaircraft batteries were deployed on both sides of the straits. Kesselring was taking no chances, as he needed the Axis forces and all their equipment to counter the next stage of the battle. The German decision to retreat was also hastened by the sudden fall from power of the Italian Fascist leader Benito Mussolini on July 25. His sudden resignation and subsequent arrest made it entirely possible that Italy would withdraw from the war. To avoid that eventuality, the Germans prepared to seize power in Italy, and that meant withdrawing quickly and efficiently from Sicily.

U.S. forces entered Messina on the evening of August 16 when a fighting patrol from the 3rd Division became the first Allied formation to enter the shattered city, two hours ahead of a British commando force. The next day, a triumphant Patton arrived at Messina, riding in a staff car sporting a three-star pennant with a small convoy behind. At the same time, Montgomery's forces had pushed north from Catania to complete the operation and but for the road being broken at Taormina, the British 50th Division might have arrived simultaneously with the U.S. forces, which would have taken some of the gloss off Patton's triumph.

It had taken the Allies the better part of a month to complete the invasion of Sicily, longer than anyone had expected, and it had been a hard slog. Much of the fighting was over difficult terrain in sweltering weather conditions, and the enemy, particularly the German panzer soldiers, had proved formidable opponents. The end results were that Sicily became a jumping-off point for the forthcoming invasion of Italy, the lines of communication through the Mediterranean were secured, and 160,000 Axis troops were killed or taken prisoner. But the victory had come at a price. Kesselring's evacuation plan worked brilliantly, allowing 40,000 German and 62,000 Italian troops to escape over the Strait of Messina, along with most of their heavy equipment. While Patton was pressing ahead to the port, the imperturbable Germans began an audacious maneuver to transfer men and equipment using a fleet of ferries and landing craft to pull their forces out from under the Allies' noses. Despite the attentions of the Royal Air Force, only seven ferries and a handful of minor vessels were sunk—a tribute to the intensity and accuracy of the antiaircraft defenses—and to make matters worse, Admiral Cunningham's warships failed to mount any interdiction missions. Given the fact that the Germans were prepared to sacrifice Sicily to the Allies in advance of the defense of Italy, their successful fighting retreat from Messina helped to turn defeat into a victory of sorts.

By allowing the enemy to retreat so easily from the island, Operation Husky was not an unalloyed success, and all the German divisions were able to take part in the next phase of the operations in Italy. If the Allies had launched the assault two months earlier, they would not have faced the kind of determined opposition that halted the Eighth Army as it fought its way through the plain of Catania. There was still much to learn about Allied cooperation and the need to maintain a unified command on the battlefield without letting matters of national pride interfere. However, it would be wrong to write off the operation as a moderate success that achieved few strategic gains in return for a substantial deployment. Montgomery's plans for the landings at Gela and Syracuse were a useful forerunner for the cross-Channel operations of the following year, and important lessons were learned about airborne operations. Once again the Germans had suffered defeat, and their panzer forces were seen to be vulnerable. Most importantly of all, from the Allies' point of view, the U.S. Army emerged as a first-class fighting force, displaying mobility, aggression, and a will to win—virtues which would stand it in good stead in the later fighting in Europe.

CHAPTER EIGHT

The Invasion of Europe

MANY OF THE COMMAND AND CONTROL PROBLEMS THAT HAD BEDEVILED the Sicilian campaign were carried over to the Allied invasion of Italy, which began in September 1943. General Harold Alexander remained in command of the 15th Army Group, and Montgomery commanded the British Eighth Army, while Lieutenant General Mark Clark commanded the U.S. Fifth Army, which included British X Corps. The plan was for the British to land at Reggio Calabria on the other side of the Strait of Messina (Operation Slapstick) while Clark's army landed south of Naples at Salerno (Operation Avalanche). Both invasions enjoyed mixed fortunes. The British landed unopposed, but Clark's army encountered stubborn resistance from German land and air forces, and only intervention by the Royal Navy allowed the landing to proceed by the middle of the month. Although both armies then made progress in their advance northward, lack of firm operational planning meant that the campaign quickly devolved into a slog. Bad weather also wreaked havoc in the advance to the Garigliano and Sangro rivers, leaving Montgomery to complain to the Chief of the Imperial General Staff (CIGS), Alan Brooke, that there could be no hope of immediate progress in the near future. An absence of realizable goals and the use of inchoate tactics caused the Italian campaign to founder. There was no timetable; attacks were uncoordinated; the German defenders fought with unexpected tenacity; and the mountainous terrain favored the defenders. Offensive operations came to a virtual halt with the onset of winter at the end of the year. Slowly the Allies were being sucked into a war of attrition, a possibility that Montgomery had noted in his diary on September 20. The Allies had, he wrote, "embarked on a major campaign on the continent of EUROPE, without having any clear idea—or plan—as to how they would develop the operations and fight the land battle." He also offered the sardonic comment that his Eighth Army would probably be asked to relieve the situation.[1]

There is more to the latter comment than injured pride. Although Montgomery has been criticized for the methodical and ponderous way in which he directed the Eighth Army in the aftermath of El Alamein, he had achieved all the objectives given to him. North Africa had been cleared of enemy forces, and Sicily had been captured, and the instrument of success had largely been the Eighth Army and its commander. On the other hand, Montgomery had been hampered by vague and frequently contradictory orders from 15th Army Group headquarters. By trying to be all things to all people, Alexander had lost control of those under his command and frequently displayed an alarming lack of "grip" on what was actually happening on the battlefield. This had been the case in Sicily, and the Italian campaign showed that little had changed. In a later appreciation, written from Italy in November, Montgomery remarked of his former student at Staff College, "ALEXANDER is my great friend. But he does not understand the business, and he is not clever; he cannot grasp the essentials."[2]

To be fair to Alexander, one of the reasons for the lull in the fighting lay in the need to build up forces and equipment for an invasion of France, which was planned for early summer in the following year. Montgomery had been asked to withdraw seven of his divisions by autumn so that they could begin training for the forthcoming battle in France. Once again, there was a divergence of opinion among the Combined Chiefs of Staff, with U.S. General George Marshall fretting that resources would be diverted, while Brooke argued that Rome would never be taken without concentrated effort. It is hard to avoid the impression that, as 1943 drew to a close, Italy was gradually taking a backseat to the invasion of France and that both Montgomery and Clark were stymied by the indecision in Washington and London.

While the planning for the French invasion (Operation Overlord) continued apace, no immediate decision was made as to who would act as commander in chief, adding to uncertainty in the British and U.S. camps. As late as November, when the Allied leadership met again in Tehran in Persia (Iran), the Soviet leader Joseph Stalin asked who would command Overlord and was told only that an announcement was imminent. There were several front-runners, all of whom had a viable claim—Marshall among them. As the United States was increasingly becoming the senior coalition partner in terms of the size of its contribution, there were grounds for awarding the post to him. If that were to come to pass, Marshall would almost certainly have been replaced as Chief of Staff to the U.S. Army by General Dwight Eisenhower, creating a vacancy in the Mediterranean command.

Then there were the claims of the British. In fact, as early as the summer of 1943, Churchill had offered the post to Brooke, even though the prime minister was in no position to make such a proposition. In any case, "Brookie" was not wholly amenable to the Americans, who mistakenly believed him to be opposed to a cross-Channel invasion. (He was in fact only opposed to the ambitious timetable, not to the operation itself).

Eventually, shortly before Christmas 1943, and after a good deal of horse trading and taking into account President Roosevelt's concerns about losing the experienced Marshall as his principal war planner, the appointment was given to Eisenhower. Montgomery was given command of the 21st Army Group, becoming the de facto commander of land forces, while the naval and air commanders were, respectively, Admiral Sir Bertram Ramsay of the Royal Navy and Air Marshal Sir Trafford Leigh-Mallory of the Royal Air Force. At the same time, Eisenhower appointed Air Chief Marshal Sir Arthur Tedder as his deputy supreme commander, in recognition of the large role to be played by the Allied air forces.

Throughout this period of tension and delay, Montgomery had been filled with apprehension that the land forces appointment would be given to Alexander, who was considered to be something of a favorite with Churchill. While that was true—as late as January 1945 the British prime minister wanted Alexander to replace Tedder, but this proposal was wisely deflected—Churchill also recognized that Montgomery had delivered him a string of victories, and the prime minister had always favored a warrior spirit in his senior commanders. Montgomery, however, had also to overcome the suspicions of Eisenhower, who was aghast at the suggestion that he should become his land forces commander, preferring Alexander, with whom he had a good relationship. He also probably believed—not without reason—that the charming and instinctively loyal Alexander would have made a reliable and consensual subordinate, unlike the prickly and opinionated Montgomery, whom Eisenhower believed to be greatly overrated as a battlefield commander.

In the end, the decision lay in Brooke's hands, as by mid-December Churchill, who had been incapacitated by exhaustion, was still undecided. On December 11, Brooke visited Eisenhower in Tunis to discuss future progress. At this meeting Eisenhower endorsed the appointment of General Sir Henry Maitland "Jumbo" Wilson as the senior commander in the Mediterranean theater but proposed that Montgomery should take over the 15th Army Group while Alexander commanded Overlord land forces. In his diary, Brooke wrote that he "didn't mind much" who was appointed, but in a later entry he changed his mind.

> It was very useful being able to have this discussion with Ike in which I discovered, as I had expected, that he would sooner have Alex with him for Overlord than Monty. He also knew that he could handle Alex, but was not fond of Monty and certainly did not know how to handle him. I am surprised that in my diary I wrote that between the selection of Alex or Monty "I don't mind much"! I certainly minded a great deal and would have little confidence in Alex running that show.[3]

Given the interest that Brooke had always taken in Montgomery's career and his protectiveness when things went wrong, it would have been surprising if he had not supported his protégé. Crucially, this appointment was also endorsed by Sir James Grigg, the Secretary of State for War. And so it came about, shortly before Christmas, that Montgomery was informed of the decision for him to command the 21st Army Group.

To those who knew the new commander's methods, it came as no surprise that Montgomery did not let the grass grow under his feet. On December 23, he wrote to Brooke, outlining his wishes for his new command to ensure that he got the pick of his favorite staff officers from the Eighth Army. Four days later he flew to confer with Churchill in Marrakech before returning to London. Typical for Montgomery, he used his time with the British prime minister to promote his own ideas for Overlord.

◈

The decision to press ahead with the invasion of northwest Europe had been made at the Trident Conference in Washington in May 1943 and planning for it began under joint U.S.-British direction immediately after the summit had ended. The main architect was British Lieutenant-General Sir Frederick Morgan, who headed a coalition planning group known as "Cossac" after the acronym for his own appointment (Chief of Staff to the Supreme Allied Commander). The main *desiderata* for the cross-Channel amphibious attack were quickly established: a landing area with unobstructed, shallow beaches within range of Allied airpower; the neutralization of local defenses to allow a buildup equal to the strength of the German defenders; and the presence of large port for reinforcement and resupply. Deception also formed part of the plan, in the form of Operation Cockade: the idea was to persuade the German high command that the assault would be made across the narrowest part of the English Channel, at Pas de Calais, where the beaches were shallow and led into the hinterland without cliffs or high ground. It also offered the opportunity make a quick strike into the Low Countries, and from there into Germany. All those reasons made Pas de Calais the ideal invasion site, but it was quickly discounted as the Allied planners knew that Rommel would deploy the bulk of their defensive forces to the most obvious location. (The German general had taken command of Army Group B, responsible for the defense of France, in November 1943.)

Morgan's plan was shown to the Allied leadership at the Quadrant Conference in Quebec at the end of the summer of 1943, and the detailed planning was then passed to the commanders of the sea, land, and air forces taking part. The chosen landing ground was the Baie de la Seine, in Normandy between Le Havre and the Cotentin Peninsula, an area that met all the criteria, including a deep-water port at Cherbourg. Until it could be secured, the Allies planned to use artificial harbors known as Mulberries, and fuel would be piped across the Channel through an undersea pipeline known as "Pluto" (for "pipe line under the ocean"). The plan called for an invasion force of three divisions, plus airborne forces, that would create a bridgehead to Normandy and Brittany. Success would depend on the ability of the Allies to build up forces more rapidly than the Germans, and with that in mind it would be essential to destroy their road and rail communications in northern France.

Upon becoming the supreme commander, Eisenhower insisted that General Walter Bedell Smith should become his chief of staff, and this appointment meant that Morgan had to be sidelined. Although he was given a subsidiary role, Eisenhower always insisted that without Morgan's efforts the D-Day operation would have been impossible. Montgomery was considerably more brutal in his approach to Cossac's work. On first reading Morgan's plan while staying with Churchill, he declared that it would not work and was doomed to failure. He also felt that it lacked grip and contained too many potential tactical shortcomings to have any chance of succeeding. As things stood at the end of 1943, the initial planning called for an invasion force of three divisions plus airborne forces that would create a bridgehead through which reinforcements could be landed quickly to break out into Normandy and Brittany. Success would depend on the ability of the Allies to build up forces more rapidly than the Germans could, and with that in mind it would be essential to deny the enemy the chance to reinforce the landing grounds by destroying road and rail communications in northern France.

It was at this stage, 18 months into the planning process, that Montgomery arrived in London, determined to make his mark on the Cossac staff.

The first meeting took place on January 3, 1944. Its location could not have been better suited—St. Paul's School, Montgomery's alma mater—and he approached the issue with an appropriately schoolmasterly way. Two of Morgan's staff officers made the initial presentation, and when they had finished, Montgomery asked for a short break before taking the floor and disagreeing with just about everything that had been said. Although he concurred with the main principles, he put forward an alternative proposal to attack with greater weight along a broader front and with a larger airborne contribution. He was concerned about the narrowness of the primary assault and suggested that the invasion should be extended west into Brittany and eastward toward the port of Dieppe.

This latter point was initially rejected by Admiral Ramsay, because he could not guarantee full naval support; but during the second day of the conference, it was agreed to extend the western landing to the Cotentin Peninsula (Utah Beach) to break out toward Cherbourg in the north and Avranches in the south, while the eastern landing would aim to take Caen. It was also agreed that the initial assault should be made by five divisions—two American, two British, and one Canadian, each with their own landing beach—with one British and two U.S. airborne divisions operating on the flanks. The main problem would be finding sufficient landing craft to mount the assault, which meant that the operation could not take place until June at the earliest. The planners then produced a new outline for Overlord based on Montgomery's proposals. A month later Eisenhower activated his headquarters as planning continued for Operation Neptune, the name given to the assault phase.

Once again Montgomery had played a decisive role in changing an invasion plan he deemed unworkable. While Eisenhower shared Montgomery's fears and General Omar Bradley, the U.S. First Army commander, also doubted the viability of Cossac's plan, it was left to Montgomery to effect the changes. In so doing, he restored a good deal of self-confidence and morale among the senior commanders who would be leading the operations. As Max Hastings, a leading historian of Operation Overlord, put it:

> After months of havering among staff officers fatally hampered by lack of authority, he [Montgomery] had sketched the design for a feasible operation of war, and begun to exercise his own immense strength of will to ensure that the resources would be found to land five divisions and secure a beachhead large enough to provide fighting room for the Allied armies.[4]

Montgomery also used his authority to redefine the landing's order of battle, which he insisted should be under his personal control. The Americans would land on the western flank and proceed to capture Cherbourg, Brest, and the Loire ports, while the British and Canadians would deal with the bulk of the enemy forces in the south and east.

Montgomery's thinking on his own role was put forward to his corps and divisional commanders on January 13, in the same location at St. Paul's School. It was startlingly simple, which is one of the reasons why Bradley and others were happy to accept Montgomery's revised plans:

> We must stop experimenting and prepare for battle. I will lay down the general form; everyone must accept it and act on it; all bellyaching will cease. You must give me your confidence. American doctrine their own affair and General Bradley will act as he thinks most suitable. The British and Canadian Armies will do as I say.[5]

The following day Montgomery set off to "binge up" the coalition troops. His first stop was the U.S. First Army; it was also the first occasion when a British commander in chief had addressed American forces. Despite his initial nervousness and some lingering hostility from American soldiers who were unsure of the general's identity, it was counted a success. Montgomery had an easy way with conscript soldiers, most of whom had never seen action, and his message was simple and honest: Let's train hard, fight to the best of our abilities, support each other in the field, and then return to our loved ones, proud that the enemy has been defeated. Montgomery could appear unprepossessing with his informal uniform and slight stature, but he was a good speaker and had a knack for getting his message across to the soldiers who would do the fighting for him. Few who heard him were left unimpressed by the experience. Even Bradley, who later became a bitter enemy, was dumbfounded by the adulation received by "the slight erect figure of Montgomery in his baggy and unpressed corduroys":

> Psychologically, the choice of Montgomery as British commander for the OVERLORD assaults came as stimulant to us all. For the thin, ascetic face that stared from an unmilitary turtle-neck sweater had, in a little over a year, become a symbol of victory in the eyes of the Allied world. Nothing becomes a general more than success in battle, and Montgomery wore success with such chipper faith in

the arms of Britain that he was cherished by a British people wearied of valorous setbacks.[6]

However, in spite of the progress being made, there were still problems to be addressed. The first was the exact nature of Montgomery's position. In his own mind he believed that Eisenhower had entrusted him with overall command of the Allied armies for the assault phase of the operation, but this grated on public opinion in the United States. While Eisenhower was the supreme commander, and U.S. personnel and equipment put the Allies' overall numbers ahead of the Germans', the naval, land, and air forces were all under British command. The matter was aired again at Eisenhower's first meeting of staff and commanders on January 21, when it was agreed that command of the ground forces would remain in Montgomery's hands for an indefinite length of time. However, the agreement was not enough to prevent later claims and recriminations about the precise roles played by the senior commanders during the operation.

The second issue centered on Montgomery's plans for Caen, the main town and communications center along the line of attack. He saw this as being the responsibility of the British and Canadian forces, which would create a protective shield on the left (or eastern) flank while the U.S. forces took on Cherbourg and led the breakout into Brittany. As reinforcements built up, the U.S. forces would then swing eastward toward the Seine and Paris. That thinking made sense, as the British and Canadian forces could protect the landings from the expected German counterattack from Pas de Calais. When that happened, Caen was bound to become the battlefront's "hinge," to be secured as quickly as possible. If it remained in German hands, there would be no access to the flatlands to the south as far as Falaise, which the Allies intended to use as a lodgment area for the buildup of forces after the landings. From the outset, therefore, Caen was regarded as a primary objective that had to be taken on the first day of the invasion.

It was a gamble, and its success was central to Montgomery's strategy. Two days later, the revised plan was approved by Eisenhower.

To put it into operation, Montgomery surrounded himself with soldiers in whom he had the greatest confidence—men who had served with him in Eighth Army. Freddie de Guingand was recalled to serve as his chief of staff, and he was joined by other first-rate talents, such as the youthful Brigadier "Bill" Williams (intelligence), Major-General Charles Richardson (plans), Major-General R. F. K. Belchem (operations) and Lieutenant-Colonel Christopher "Kit" Dawnay (military assistant). Montgomery also earmarked his favorite formations, including the 7th Armoured and 51st (Highland) Divisions, as central to his planning. Such favoritism is not unusual among senior commanders in high-stakes operations, and Montgomery was absolutely ruthless in getting his own way. The removal of deadwood inevitably caused hard feelings and created long-lasting resentment, but the new commander was not slow in making his presence felt at headquarters. "We never lost confidence in him," said one of his staff officers, "but we would very often say: 'Oh Christ, what's the little bugger doing now?'"[7]

The timetable for Overlord was tight and left little room for maneuver or last-minute changes. Montgomery insisted that all planning had to be complete by the end of March, leaving April for intensive training, with a full-scale rehearsal at the beginning of May. On April 7, again within the confines of St. Paul's School, Montgomery summoned his senior field officers for a presentation in which he outlined the different phases of the operation. Those who had served in North Africa remembered that he brought to the occasion the same quiet determination and professionalism as he had to a similar conference ahead of the Battle of El Alamein. The timing of the operation was fixed for the first full moon in June.

In Montgomery's view the battle would run through three phases lasting up to 80 days. The first would run for 20 days and would see the U.S. First Army capturing its objectives in the Cotentin Peninsula, while the British Second Army (led by Lieutenant-General Sir Miles Dempsey) assaulted west of the Orne River, pivoting on Caen to shield the U.S. offensive. Phase Two would be the beginning of the breakout, with the British forces pushing south through Falaise toward Argentan, while the Americans moved toward the Loire and Quiberon Bay. Phase Three would take the Allies to the Seine, with the U.S. First Army heading to Paris, while the British and Canadians would operate to the north between Rouen and the Channel. At the same time, Patton's U.S. Third Army would move through the First Army's front to clear Brittany and then assume posts on the southern flank.

It was all very neat and all orderly, but the truth was that a battle of this magnitude could not be fought in such a precise fashion, and it was obvious that Montgomery's so-called phase lines would not survive the first enemy contact. Bradley, in particular, was infuriated by the proposals and demanded the deletion of phase lines in the U.S. sector. Although the concept was stricken from the final briefing to senior commanders on May 15, the course of the battle unfolded very much as Montgomery predicted, despite the expected setbacks along the way. If Montgomery did make any mistakes during this final planning conference—which, like its predecessor was judged a brilliant performance—it lay in his supreme self-confidence and his absolute mastery of the plan. At that stage of the war, no other Allied commander could have refined and revised the plan and succeeded in selling his colleagues on it, but Montgomery's certainty made him a hostage of fortune, and many of his claims would come back to haunt him.

The opening months of 1944 were nevertheless a key moment in Montgomery's career as a general. The storming of Normandy became known as D-Day and launched the invasion of Nazi-controlled Europe in June 1944, the beginning of the end of Hitler's regime. We have become so used to celebrating the success of the great Allied operation, however, that it is quite easy to forget the narrowness of the margin of success. Right up to the final moments, Eisenhower was by no means convinced that the operation would succeed—he even wrote a press release to be made available in the event of failure—and both Brooke and Churchill shared his occasional pessimism.[8] So much depended on air superiority and getting as many men and as much equipment ashore as quickly as possible; meteorological conditions also came into play. A prompter and more determined response by Rommel could have driven the Allied armies back into the Channel, for example. If that had happened, the disaster would have set back the Allied cause for many years, and, with the Red Army advancing inexorably in the east, it would have changed both the course of the war and the peace that followed. The success of Montgomery's plan was as important as that.

Peacetime soldiering: formal portrait of Montgomery while commanding 1st Royal Warwickshire Regiment between 1931 and 1934. (Imperial War Museum IWM MH22844)

Shortly after taking over command of the British Eighth Army, Montgomery (bare headed) gives directions to Brigadier "Pip" Roberts (wearing black beret). Lieutenant-General Brian Horrocks stands to Montgomery's right. (Imperial War Museum IWM E15788)

One of the most striking photographs of the Second World War, taken in the aftermath of the British victory at El Alamein in November 1942. Wearing his trademark black beret, Montgomery watches the beginning of the German retreat from the turret of a Grant tank. (Imperial War Museum IWM E18980)

While at home on leave in Britain, Montgomery helped the British war effort by giving stirring addresses to the civilian workforce. He is speaking in a factory "somewhere in Britain" in 1943. (Imperial War Museum IWM P1917)

Group photograph at Allied headquarters in Algiers in June 1943. Seated from left to right: British Foreign Secretary Anthony Eden, General Sir Alan Brooke, British Prime Minister Winston Churchill and U.S. Generals George C. Marshall and Dwight D. Eisenhower. Montgomery is standing at right. (Imperial War Museum IWM NA3286)

During all his operations, Montgomery understood the need to keep the press informed of what he was doing. Talking to war correspondents in Normandy shortly after the D-Day landings in June 1944. (Imperial War Museum IWM B5530)

In common with most British soldiers, Montgomery was very fond of pet animals and took his terrier puppies on campaign with him in France. They were named "Hitler" and "Rommel," and in the background can be seen a cage of canaries. (Imperial War Museum IWM B6541)

With U.S. Major General Matthew B. Ridgway, commander of 18th U.S. Airborne Division, during the Battle of the Bulge in the winter of 1944–1945. Montgomery frequently clashed with his U.S. opposite numbers, and his appointment to command U.S. troops on the northern flank of the German salient was considered controversial. (Imperial War Museum IWM EA49926)

Three Allied generals with their trademark uniforms: Montgomery in black beret, General Omar N. Bradley (center) in steel helmet, and Lieutenant General George S. Patton with ivory-handled revolver. (Imperial War Museum IWM B6551)

The first meeting between Montgomery (center) and Bradley on French soil after the successful D-Day landings in Normandy, June 1944. To Montgomery's left is Lieutenant-General Miles C. Dempsey, commanding the British Second Army. (Imperial War Museum IWM B5323)

Montgomery's finest hour: German plenipotentiaries arrive at his headquarters in north Germany to seek surrender terms on May 3, 1945. (Imperial War Museum IWM BU5141)

An informal portrait of Field Marshal Montgomery as Chief of the Imperial General Staff in his office at the War Office in London, October 1947. (Imperial War Museum IWM MH774)

CHAPTER NINE

Normandy: From D-Day to Deadlock

RIGHT UP TO THE LAST MINUTE, UNCERTAIN WEATHER CONDITIONS IN THE English Channel placed a question mark over the precise timing of the Allied invasion of Europe. Montgomery wanted to keep to the agreed date, June 5, but was rightly overruled by Eisenhower, who insisted on a 24-hour postponement to await the outcome of a summer storm. On the eve of the operation, Montgomery visited officers and men of D Company, 2nd Oxfordshire and Buckinghamshire Light Infantry, 6th Airborne Division, who would be among the first Allied soldiers to land in France, in their case in Horsa gliders. His words to Major John Howard, the commanding officer, say much about Montgomery and his approach to warfare: "Bring back as many of the chaps as you can."[1] Hours later, on June 6, Howard's company fired the first shots of Operation Overlord when they engaged German sentries guarding two bridges on the Orne River and Caen Canal shortly after midnight. Although casualties would mount later in the day, both of those objectives were secured with few losses. As it turned out, by the end of D-Day (the first day of the operation), casualties were much lower than had been feared. Despite encountering fierce opposition at Omaha Beach, the U.S. First Army's landing ground, the for-the-most-part Allied forces got safely ashore, and the losses in personnel at the end of that first day were fewer than 10,000 killed, wounded, or missing. Meanwhile, more than 156,000 soldiers had made it ashore, and it seemed that the German defenders had been taken completely by surprise.

Montgomery made the crossing on board the destroyer HMS *Faulknor* and went straight to bed at 9:30 P.M. The following morning, U.S. General Omar Bradley arrived from his command ship, the USS *Aurora,* in order to discuss the difficulties on Omaha, and it was agreed that the planned U.S. move to Cherbourg would be delayed while the attacking British divisions extended their western flank to offer protection against any German counterattack. On the morning of June 8, after another night at sea, Montgomery went ashore to assess progress. In spite of the initial difficulties, the U.S. forces had made good progress at Omaha, on the eastern flank the port of Ouistreham was in Allied hands, and Bayeux was under siege— but worryingly, the German 21st Panzer Division had seized Caen. Undaunted, Montgomery ordered the British land forces commander Lieutenant-General Miles Dempsey to recapture it by envelopment before the Germans could mount a counterattack. Remembering the fluidity of desert warfare, Montgomery, more than anything else at this stage, wanted to prevent Rommel from retaking the initiative to attempt to drive the Allies from their lodgment area.

He was right to be concerned. Rommel's arrival in France had galvanized the defending German forces, and although there were continuing tensions in the high command, with overall control vested in Field Marshal Gerd von Rundstedt in Paris, the eleven German armored divisions in northern France still provided formidable opposition. When the invasion began, Rommel was in fact in Germany visiting his wife, but he was back in harness late on June 6, after a 12-hour journey. Despite some confusion about the Allies' intentions—there was a belief that Normandy was a diversion and that the main attack could come to Pas de Calais—Rommel soon had a grip on the battle. Crucially, he ordered that resistance be stiffened along the front at Caen and Caumont, where the British were already discovering the difficulties posed by operating tanks in the surrounding *bocage* country, which consisted of small, irregular fields bisected by hedges and small trees.

Montgomery's plan was to envelop Caen by attacking from the right toward Villers-Bocage with the 7th Armoured Division, while the 51st (Highland) Division moved on the left flank through the Orne bridgehead to deliver a left hook on Caen. He also considered dropping the 1st Airborne Division in the center. At the Allied conference at Port-en-Bessin, Montgomery ordered the U.S. forces to move rapidly toward Cherbourg. On the evening of June 8, he informed Eisenhower that he was pleased with the way the operation was going, but already hopes of an early breakout were being dashed. Casualties were growing in the British sector, and the depth of the front was still frighteningly narrow—hence the importance of the operation to deal with the Germans currently defending Caen.

Ahead of the attack, Montgomery claimed that he was sending in his "best batsmen"—an allusion to the English love of cricket and, in this case, an indication that he would be using two divisions that had distinguished themselves as first-class assault formations in North Africa. However, in Normandy's *bocage* country, with its narrow, hedge-lined fields and sunken lanes—so different from the open spaces of the desert—they were to receive a rude shock. The 7th Armoured "Desert Rats" had fought in every major battle in North Africa, as had the 51st (Highland) Division—which, as the successors to the men forced to surrender at St. Valéry in May 1940, had a score to settle with the Germans. Montgomery thought highly of both of these divisions and had earmarked them as elite formations after they had been withdrawn from Italy the previous year.

The experience of the Highlanders of the 51st in Normandy gives some idea of the problems faced by Montgomery and the British Second Army as they grappled to gain control of the main battlefront at Caen. Touchy, irascible, clannish, and difficult to handle other than by their own officers and NCOs, the men in the division came from both Territorial and Regular regiments representing just about every part of Scotland— Black Watch from the central Highlands; Gordon Highlanders from the northeast, Seaforth and Cameron Highlanders from the north; and Argyll and Sutherland Highlanders from the western seaboard. The Highland Division had not been selected for the initial assault but formed part of the second wave that supported the D-Day landings in preparation for the expected breakout. On landing the men soon found that this was going to be very different from fighting in North Africa or Sicily, and that lesson was learned the hard way. One of the first formations ashore was The 5th Black Watch, which quickly discovered that the German defenders were determined to hold their ground and push the invading forces back toward the coast. During the first week of fighting in the operations around Colville, on the Orne River, the battalion had a total of 307 casualties—6 officers and 92 soldiers killed; 11 officers and 198 soldiers wounded. The figures were put into perspective by the battalion historian: "When compared to the 529 casualties for the whole of the North African campaign and the 11 casualties for the Sicilian campaign it gave a clear picture of the heavy price paid."[2] The 7th Black Watch fared little better, moving up to Ranville with 42 casualties, due mainly to heavy enemy machine-gun fire.

An attack on the suburb of Colombelles to the northeast of Caen on July 11 also ran into difficulties. Both the 5th and 7th Battalions of The Black Watch took part in the offensive, but the defenses were stronger, and as casualties mounted there was no option but to withdraw. The 5th Battalion suffered 128 casualties, including 71 killed or missing. After that failure, it became clear that the 51st (Highland) Division was exhausted and had lost much of its fighting spirit. Not everyone was affected, but all the indications point to a disastrous drop in morale among the frontline soldiers. Before the Colombelles attack, Major Alexander Brodie, commanding A Company of the 5th Battalion Black Watch, made his feelings clear when he told his men that he "would not hesitate to shoot anyone who ran away," and that he "expected them to shoot me or any officer or NCO who ordered them to pack in."[3] This view was shared by the division's historian in his account of the battle: "A kind of claustrophobia affected the troops and the continual shelling and mortaring from an unseen enemy in relatively great strength were certainly very trying."[4]

So precipitous was the drop in morale that by mid-July, Montgomery reported to Brooke that the 51st (Highland) Division was no longer "battle worthy" and "does not fight with determination." As a result, Montgomery was forced to fire the divisional commander, Major-General Charles Bullen-Smith, on the grounds that "the men won't fight for [him.]"[5] It was a drastic measure to take in the middle of a battle, and although Montgomery was loath to make it, he had no option. Bullen-Smith was replaced by Major-General T. G. Rennie, a battle-hardened Black Watch officer who had previously commanded Montgomery's old 3rd Infantry Division. The Highlanders were taken out of the line for a short period of rest and recuperation at Cazelle, northwest of Caen, and some of the weakened battalions were reinforced with fresh soldiers, many of them from English regiments.

Thanks to its experience, though, the 51st quickly recovered its fighting form and went on to be one of the outstanding British divisions during the advance into northwest Europe. While the 51st's example and the equally demoralizing failure of the 7th Armoured Division at Villers-Bocage do not excuse the criticisms Montgomery later faced for his direction of the Caen offensive, they do give some idea of the difficulties he was facing. Despite their stellar records, both of Montgomery's favored divisions faltered in Normandy. This was due in part, no doubt, to the strength of the German opposition, but there was also a feeling among the men that they had played their part during their previous two years and now it was someone else's turn.

Leadership in the ranks was an issue as well. All too often, battalion and brigade commanders failed to use initiative and mounted their attacks "by the book," preferring a conventional set-piece battle to the kind of improvised, bloody-minded aggression employed by the Germans, many of whom were equally battle-weary after fighting against the Red Army on the eastern front. After all the meticulous training and preparation for Overlord, this was a desperate disappointment, and some of the blame must be placed on Montgomery. After the war his old colleague, the distinguished military theorist Sir Basil Liddell Hart, offered his assessment of what had gone wrong in the immediate aftermath of D-Day:

> Time after time they [British Second Army] were checked or even induced to withdraw by boldly handled pockets of Germans of inferior strength. But for our air superiority, which hampered the Germans at every turn, the results would have been much worse. Our forces seem to have had too little initiative in infiltration, and also too little determination—with certain exceptions. Repeatedly one finds that big opportunities were forfeited because crucial attacks were stopped after suffering trifling casualties. That was particularly marked with the armoured formations.[6]

Normally a good reader of his soldiers' feelings, Montgomery missed the signs, and the attack on Caen quickly faltered as a result.

To his credit he did respond quickly and effectively. It was impossible to retrain all the disaffected troops in the middle of a battle, but Montgomery was alert to the need to make changes. In addition to Bullen-Smith, Major-General Bobby Erskine of the 7th Armoured was fired, as was XXX Corps commander Lieutenant-General G. C. Bucknell, who was replaced by Horrocks. Montgomery also had to find a new plan to provide the Royal Air Force with airfields south of Caen and to increase the size of the British lodgment area. The result was Operation Goodwood, which required British VIII Corps (led by General Sir Richard O'Connor) to jump off from its bridgehead east of the Orne and to move quickly and aggressively toward Falaise. Simultaneously, Bradley's U.S. First Army would advance toward St. Lô to use it as a base for an assault to the west. Eisenhower gave the plan his full endorsement, but by that stage of the battle, the supreme commander was beginning to tire of Montgomery's inability to take Caen, a failing which he attributed to the general's extreme caution in directing the Allied armies.[7] In an attempt to dislodge the German forces in Caen, which Hitler had ordered to be defended at all costs, the RAF bombed the city heavily on the night of July 6, but it came at a cost, with an estimated 1,250 civilian casualties.

However, Goodwood was doomed to difficulties even before it began. Aerial reconnaissance had given the Germans adequate notice of the buildup of Allied armor, while British intelligence failed to accurately discern the size and depth of the defending forces. Once again bombers of the RAF and U.S. Army Air Force attacked the target area, dropping 7,567 tons of bombs along a front that stretched 7,000 yards. But despite the sound and fury, the bombardment was not wholly accurate, and important defensive positions such as the Bourguébus Ridge were left unscathed. These lapses played into the Germans' hands, and as the 11th Armoured Division commenced the attack, it quickly stalled in an uncleared minefield.

To the west, the 3rd Canadian Division also ran into difficulties near Vaucelles, where it encountered heavy resistance. All along the front line, it soon became clear that German antitank positions were still intact, especially those equipped with the dreaded 88-millimeter flak guns. Soon they were taking a heavy toll in what came to be known as the British armored divisions' "death ride." To compound the problems, at midday on June 18 the German 21st Panzer Division mounted a counterattack from the opposite slopes of the Bourguébus Ridge, wreaking havoc with the 11th Armoured Division's Sherman and Cromwell tanks. Delays and choke-points kept the 7th Armoured Division from offering any meaningful support, and to make matters worse, the 3rd Infantry's attack also faltered. At the end of a bruising day, the British and Canadians had lost almost 200 tanks and had 5,337 battlefield casualties during the course of Operation Goodwood.

❖

By Montgomery's standards, Goodwood had gone off half-cocked. After stalling on the first day, there was no chance that the tanks could break out into the open country that led to Falaise. Montgomery was right to call it off as soon as he did, to prevent needless casualties. It did not help that the weather had broken again with thunderous rainstorms hindering movement and halting air operations. The management of the aftermath, however, was badly handled. In a signal to Brooke, Montgomery spoke of "a complete success...situation very promising and it is difficult to see what the enemy can do at present."[8] The embedded war correspondents were briefed that the operation had been a success and that all objectives had been achieved, but this was a far cry from the earlier claims that the massive breakout would open the way to Paris.[9]

There was consternation in the Allied high command at what had transpired. Following his earlier optimism, Eisenhower was deeply disappointed, especially after the bad weather also forced the postponement of Bradley's offensive. But the most vehement criticism was expressed by the RAF's commander, Tedder, and his colleagues, Air Marshal Sir Arthur Coningham (Allied Tactical Air Force) and Air Marshal Sir Arthur Harris (Bomber Command). All three felt that Montgomery had misled them by insisting on using scarce heavy and medium bombers to support a major ground offensive. Furthermore, Caen's capture would have allowed them to set up a forward base at the Carpiquet airfield to the west of the city, which they needed to mount interdiction operations further afield. They were furious when Goodwood was shut down so quickly and made their feelings clear in the written narrative for the *Official History:* "General Montgomery was reminded that the Air Forces were relying on the early capture of terrain beyond Caen, but after a few days he appeared to be accepting the situation with something like complacency."[10]

Worse, Tedder used his position as Eisenhower's deputy to try to get Montgomery fired. On the night of July 19, he told the supreme commander that "the British Chiefs of Staff would support any recommendation that he might care to make, meaning that if Ike wanted to sack Monty for not succeeding in going places with his big three armoured division push, he would have no difficulty officially."[11] The matter was reported by Eisenhower's naval aide, Lieutenant-Commander Harry Butcher, but his account is not strictly accurate. Although Tedder was within his rights to suggest that there should be a change in field commanders, he was wrong to claim that this would be approved by Brooke. That same day Brooke had visited Montgomery at his headquarters, ostensibly to persuade him to allow Churchill to visit France (the prime minister was under the misapprehension that he had been banned), but also to offer much-needed support. His diary records what he said.

> First of all I put matter of PM's visit right by getting Monty to write a note to PM telling him that he did not know that he wanted him to come and invited him. Then warned him of tendency in PM to listen to suggestions that Monty played for safety and was not prepared to take risks, mainly fostered by Tedder egged on by Coningham.... I think these various backgrounds may assist Monty. I found him in great form and delighted with his success east of Caen.[12]

This was an extraordinary episode. In the middle of a battle in danger of reaching stalemate, senior RAF officers conspired to remove the Allies' main land commander on the grounds that he had misused air assets and shown that he was incapable of breaking the deadlock at Caen. No general's job should ever be sacrosanct, and it is of course right and proper that colleagues should voice disapproval or even demand change, but Tedder and Coningham were guilty of going behind Montgomery's back at a crucial moment.

Eventually, the criticism died down, but the affair reveals the strains in the coalition's high command. In that respect, Montgomery did not help himself by downplaying Goodwood's claims to success, and this irritated his American allies. Having forecast a breakthrough, he then attempted to sell the more limited gains of the first day as his original tactical objective. This has struck many later American commentators as a cover-up for his failure to take Caen as he had promised during the final briefing at St. Paul's School on May 15. General George Patton, typically, said as much at the time. Following a visit to Montgomery's headquarters on July 7, he noted in his diary: "Montgomery went to great lengths explaining why the British had done nothing."[13]

However, Goodwood was not a total setback. Although its full aims had not been achieved, the attack tied down German armor at a time when Bradley was preparing to launch Operation Cobra, the breakout to the west that would eventually take U.S. forces as far as Avranches. The Germans always believed that the Allies would attempt to move toward Paris by taking the Falaise route, and this led them to place the bulk of their armor on the British and Canadian flank. Seen in that light, Goodwood did serve a purpose at a difficult point in the battle for Normandy, and with the benefit of hindsight it is possible to see it for what it was: a blocking operation that removed pressure off Bradley as he moved his forces toward St. Lô ahead of one of the most astonishing moves of the Normandy campaign—Patton's rapid armored assault that moved U.S. forces into open country before the Germans had the chance to regroup. This latter operation was the only Allied use of blitzkrieg—the rapid and ruthless penetration of the enemy's lines using overwhelming force—during the Second World War.

The stalemate was broken by Operation Cobra, mounted on July 25 by the U.S. First Army, which pushed as far south as Avranches and the pivotal neighboring town of Pontaubault. Suddenly, the possibility opened up of invading Brittany in the west and racing eastward toward Le Mans and the Seine. The task was given to seven divisions of Patton's U.S. Third Army, which moved with exemplary speed into Brittany, frequently running ahead of their lines of communication as they sped into the open countryside. Bottlenecks and traffic jams were overcome by dispatching staff officers to forward positions with instructions to allow the units through, regardless of their sequence in the battle plans. Within three days, Patton's divisions were through the Avranches-Pontaubault gap. It was not a maneuver that would have been recognized at Staff College, but it worked.

Patton's breakout also altered the complexion of the battle and forced the commanders to rethink their tactics. Between them, Montgomery and Bradley agreed that the main weight of the offensive should be shifted eastward, taking the emphasis off Brittany. As Montgomery put it at the time, "Great vistas are opening up ahead, and we want Generals now who will put their heads down and go like hell."[14] With the U.S. First Army and the British and Canadian forces pushing south from their earlier confinement in Normandy—the Americans toward Vire and Mortain, Montgomery's forces toward the fracture line in the enemy lines at Falaise—there was every prospect of trapping the German Seventh and Fifth Panzer Armies, which had been ordered by Hitler to resist, whatever the cost. The Germans needed to act decisively to halt the Allied advance into their pocket—a suicidal attack on the town of Mortain was fought off by U.S. VII Corps on August 15—but their armored divisions were sorely depleted, and their infantry had suffered heavy casualties. Meanwhile, the Allies had to continue their push south and east with speed and determination if they were to cut off the German line of retreat toward the Seine.

Montgomery's response was Operation Totalise, whose object was to break through the enemy positions to the south and east of Caen and then to push on to Falaise. With the Americans steadily advancing eastward on a short hook, the two forces would meet up at Argentan to tie up the German pocket. The task was given to the Canadian First Army, reinforced by British I Corps and the recently arrived 1st Polish Armoured Division. It began before midnight on August 7, starting at the Bourguébus Ridge. This time there was no preliminary artillery, but the advance had been preceded by a RAF bombing raid that proved remarkably accurate. As the men moved forward in the darkness, their way forward was illuminated by "Monty moonlight"—searchlight beams reflected off clouds—and by guns firing tracers.

By dawn, the first objectives were taken, but then the operation faltered. A support attack by the U.S. air forces caused over 300 friendly fire casualties, and the German antitank defenses remained intact, with the result that the armored formations were at a standstill by August 11. Once more the stalemate was a test of Montgomery's credibility, especially as Operation Cobra had made such good progress. Rapid reinforcement of the Canadian corps with British armor might have resolved the issue, but that was not Montgomery's way, and the further advance was agonizingly slow. It was not until August 19 that Polish and U.S. forces met up at Chambois and the Falaise gap was slowly closed, but by then hundreds of German soldiers had made good their escape eastward, many of them experienced and battle-hardened officers and NCOs who lived to fight another day.

Just as Montgomery was held accountable for the failure to take Caen, so too was much of the blame for the delay in closing the Falaise gap laid at his feet, further staining his reputation as a battlefield commander. Bradley was particularly incensed, writing later that "a golden opportunity had truly been lost" and that he blamed Montgomery for it.[15] His thoughts were expressed with the benefit of hindsight and following further rifts between the two men later in the campaign, but the true character of the Normandy invasion was best summed up by Liddell Hart, who described it as "an operation that eventually went to plan, but not according to timetable."[16]

Overlord had been superbly planned and executed, and it remains a monument to the professionalism of Allied staff work. However, once ashore, all the armies found themselves on a steep learning curve, and both Montgomery and Bradley, as well as their field commanders, were forced to plan, fight, replan, and fight again, learning as they proceeded. Then there was the nature of the opposition. The Germans fought with a tenacity that was often frightening in its intensity, and in the Tiger tank and the 88-millimeter flak gun, they had two of the most potent weapons in the world. Nothing had prepared the Allied soldiers for all that.

CHAPTER TEN

A Lost Port and a Bridge Too Far

ON SEPTEMBER 1,1944, U.S. GENERAL DWIGHT EISENHOWER ASSUMED direct control of Allied ground forces in Europe, while General Omar N. Bradley took command of the U.S. 12th Army Group, a promotion that gave him parity with Montgomery. To help soften the blow and to emphasize the importance of Montgomery's role, that same day Winston Churchill promoted him to the rank of field marshal, the pinnacle of the profession for any British Army officer. Although the change in structure had been planned in advance, it inevitably caused turbulence within the Allied chain of command. In fact, by then, the first fissures had already appeared that would eventually sour Montgomery's relations with Eisenhower and his fellow American generals, both at the time and in the years to come. On August 23, Eisenhower had rejected Montgomery's plan for a major northern offensive that involved 40 divisions pushing toward Antwerp as a prelude to attacking the Ruhr. Instead it was agreed that U.S. and British forces would remain separate, with Montgomery's 21st Army Group taking responsibility for the northern sector, while Bradley's U.S. 12th Army Group made its eastern thrust toward the Saar, south of the Ardennes. Wherever necessary, priority would be given to the northern thrust, but this was often ignored by Bradley, who made a priority of his own operations, particularly those involving General George Patton's Third Army, which had emerged as the cutting edge of the U.S. offensive.

Later, the discussion of the two different plans came to be known as the "single thrust" versus "broad thrust" argument, with Montgomery favoring the former and Eisenhower the latter. In the postwar period, this was one of the incidents over which the generals disagreed in their memoirs. Montgomery's thinking was summed up in a paper written on August 26 entitled "Notes on Future Operations," in which he argued for a concentration of Allied effort:

> The quickest way to win this war is for the great mass of the Allied armies to advance northwards, clear the coast as far as Antwerp, establish a powerful air force in Belgium, and advance into the Ruhr.... The force must operate as one whole, with great cohesion and so strong that it can do the job quickly.[1]

There was much good sense in this approach. Montgomery believed that a potent, concentrated attack would quickly penetrate German defenses, while a broad front approach would dissipate resources. However, by then he was no longer in ascendance. There was a new supreme commander in Eisenhower, and Bradley and Patton were full of self-confidence following the U.S. Army's aggressive and successful breakout from Normandy. The American commanders could not help noting that during the Normandy operations the British had moved slowly and cautiously, so much so that they doubted Montgomery's capacity to do the job quickly. Even Churchill was forced to concede later in life that the balance of power had changed, telling his wartime doctor, Lord Moran, "Up to July 1944 England had a considerable say in things: after that I was conscious that it was America who made the big decisions."[2] Politics also intruded. Despite considerable provocation from Montgomery and Patton, Eisenhower was determined to maintain the integrity of the coalition and refused to favor any of his subordinate commanders. Besides, he had another problem to face—he needed to supply and resupply his forces as they made their way into the French heartland.

As the Allied armies started moving away from the landing grounds, their supply lines became longer, and that had an inevitable impact on the speed of their advance into northwest Europe. It also meant that the war would not end in 1944, thus dashing the hopes of thousands of Allied soldiers who believed that Germany was on the brink of defeat following Normandy. Some had even dared to hope that the war might be over by Christmas. Even Bradley's aide-de-camp, Colonel Chester Hansen, reckoned that the Germans were on the point of surrender as there was "no resistance of any moment in front of us."[3]

The Germans, of course, thought otherwise. On September 3, Field Marshal Walter Model, who had succeeded Field Marshal Gunther von Kluge in command of Army Group B, issued an order of the day reminding his men that while they had lost a battle they could still win the war.

The following day, his words came back to haunt him when it seemed all too possible that Montgomery had played an unexpected masterstroke. The morning of September 4, the first units of the 11th Armoured Division entered the Belgian port of Antwerp, having faced little or no resistance along the way. British commanders were jubilant, not just because they had achieved an easy victory, but because the capture of the port would solve all the Allied supply problems: Antwerp could handle 40,000 tons of supplies a day; it had 10 square miles of docks, 20 miles of waterfront, and 600 cranes. But there was a downside—Antwerp was about 80 miles from the open sea on the Scheldt River, and along that route lay the islands of Walcheren and

North and South Beveland, all held by the Germans, who were in a good position to disrupt the flow of shipping into the port.

Members of the Belgian resistance urged the British to push north to secure the Scheldt and the islands, with their strategically important access to the Netherlands. But while the British armored regiments refueled and regrouped, the German 15th Army recovered from the stunning surprise by securing Walcheren. During the next two weeks they employed a variety of ships and ferries to transport 65,000 soldiers, 225 artillery pieces, and 750 vehicles across the Scheldt, where they were able to make good their escape into the Netherlands. At the same time, they blew up the important bridges over the Albert Canal, another vital escape route. Although the German movements were known to the Allies through Ultra decrypts, it took time for the Allied high command to bolster the 11th Armoured Division, and in that period the Germans regained the initiative by pushing reinforcements into the area. Long after the war had ended, the historian of 11th Armoured Division admitted that it had been in a position to attempt to prevent the German moves, but no orders were given, and the chance was lost.[4] It was not until September 13, nine days later, that the task of clearing the Scheldt was given to weakened Canadian I Corps, but even then there was a delay. The Germans had taken full advantage of the opening, and as the war correspondent Chester Wilmot noted, their energy and ingenuity in exploiting the terrain would cause the Allies all manner of problems in the weeks that lay ahead:

> Between this water barrier [Albert Canal] and the next [Meuse-Escaut Canal] the terrain lent itself to defence, for it is sandy heath broken by small streams and patches of swamp. Here the Germans concentrated on holding the main crossroads, establishing themselves in stoutly-built villages which were difficult to by-pass and which could not be quickly taken by direct assault since the [Allied] armoured divisions had not sufficient infantry or artillery. The defenders, mostly from parachute regiments, fought with fanatical

bravery and were dislodged only when their village strongholds were demolished house by house.[5]

Later, in his memoirs, Montgomery admitted that it was "a bad mistake on my part—I underestimated the difficulties of opening up the approaches to Antwerp.... I reckoned the Canadian Army could do it while we were going for the Ruhr. I was wrong."[6] However, at the time it was clear that Montgomery had taken his eye off the ball by concentrating on advancing to the Rhine, and in so doing, had contributed to a serious blunder in prosecuting the final stages of the war. Eisenhower at Supreme Headquarters Allied Expeditionary Force (SHAEF) headquarters must also shoulder some of the blame, being responsible for all operational matters, but as Montgomery was in command of the northern 21st Army Group, the buck must stop with him.

There are several reasons for this failure. Montgomery was still preoccupied with the broad-versus-narrow front disagreement with Eisenhower and used the capture of Antwerp to press his idea of concentrating Allied forces for a massed attack on Berlin. In fact, his argument was strengthened by the Antwerp capture. The German Fifteenth Army had been isolated, and the Allies had a superior tank force at their disposal in Belgium—eight British armored divisions, one of which, Guards Armoured, had captured Brussels—which could all be supported by superior airpower. As there was only enough transport and fuel for one thrust, it made sense to divert the resources north toward the Ruhr.

But such a move needed decisiveness and speed. Although there was much to commend in Montgomery's argument, he had underestimated the weakness of the German position once the 11th Armoured Division seized Antwerp. A visit to the area might have changed his perspective, because Montgomery was a master at grasping the importance of pivotal strategic objectives, but he didn't go there. Then, when he attempted to reverse the situation, he used a formation that required reinforcement by British and Polish troops—taking three weeks—and was commanded by a general whom he did not trust. Montgomery had already lambasted the lack of leadership shown by Lieutenant-General Henry Crerar, and the matter was not resolved until September 27 when Crerar fell ill and was invalided back to Britain.

When Canadian I Corps was eventually up to strength, it took two months to secure the Scheldt, which should have been completed a few days after Antwerp fell into Allied hands during the late summer months. In this instance it is hard to avoid the conclusion that Montgomery failed to move decisively at a time when the German forces were at their weakest. As it turned out, the subsequent fighting on the Scheldt was some of the toughest in northwest campaign, with 13,000 casualties, the majority Canadian. Tanks were superfluous given the watery terrain, but great use was made of amphibious vehicles, and most of the time the Allied infantrymen were operating below sea level. (Ironically, one of the reinforcements, 52nd [Lowland] Division, had been trained specifically for mountain warfare.) It was not until November 28 that the first transport ships were able to enter the Scheldt estuary to begin bringing in much-needed supplies for the Allied armies. By then it had become all too clear that the war would continue into the following year.

There was another reason for Montgomery's lack of control during the advance toward Antwerp: his mind had wandered onto other possibilities. Since the beginning of September he had been looking for an opportunity to break the stalemate by deploying the First Allied Airborne Army (commanded by Lieutenant-General Lewis H. Brereton) to cut off the German retreat or to secure advance positions ahead of the ground forces. There was also another strategic imperative. In the summer of 1944, the Germans fired the first upgraded V-2 bombardment rocket against London and started using them against Allied forces in Antwerp as well. Launched from small, concealed sites on the northern Dutch coast, it was essential to neutralize the threat as quickly as possible. That provoked Montgomery into developing a plan to outflank the Germans by establishing a bridgehead across the lower Rhine at the Dutch town of Arnhem. Using airborne and armored forces, the attack would be made through the Netherlands to secure bridges over the Rhine between Wesel and Arnhem and then to open a path into the Ruhr.

The result was a plan called "Operation Market-Garden"—Market being the air component whereby airborne forces would seize the bridges across eight strategic waterways, while Garden had Horrocks's XXX Corps racing across them, covering 59 miles in three days from the start line on the Meuse-Escaut Canal. The bulk of the First Allied Airborne Army would be used: the U.S. 101st Airborne Division would land between Eindhoven and Veghel; the U.S. 82nd Airborne Division would be dropped around Grave and Groesbeek; and the British 1st Airborne Division would tackle Arnhem. Altogether there would be 16,500 parachute troops and 3,500 airborne troops landing by gliders.

At a September 10 meeting in Brussels, Eisenhower accepted the plan and ordered Lieutenant-General Brereton to "operate in support of the Northern Group of Armies up to and including the crossing of the Rhine."[7] However, while the matter was being discussed, Eisenhower had to endure a bad-tempered explosion from Montgomery criticizing the strategic thinking. Another commander in chief might have fired his unruly subordinate for insolence, but Eisenhower was equal to the task. Putting his hand on Montgomery's knee, he said simply but witheringly, "Steady, Monty, you can't speak to me like that. I'm your boss."[8] It had the desired effect. Montgomery apologized and continued with the discussion of the plans for Market-Garden.

Initially, Eisenhower was not of a mind to give priority to the operation, but two days later, when it became clear that Patton's push to the Saar had stalled, he dispatched Walter Bedell Smith to the 21st Army Group headquarters to consent to Montgomery's recommendation that strategic supplies should be diverted to the airborne and ground operations for a limited period. That evening Montgomery sent a signal to Brooke confirming the agreement. "So we have gained a great victory. I feel somewhat exhausted by it all but hope we shall now win the war reasonably quickly."[9]

Eisenhower quickly responded with a signal that "these measures are emergency ones and must be temporary"—but Montgomery's tail was up, and he believed that nothing could stop him from establishing the bridgehead that would provide a jumping-off point for capturing the Ruhr and shortening the war. D-Day for the operations was fixed for September 17, and planning was put in the hands of Lieutenant-General Frederick "Boy" Browning, a Guards officer who had achieved minor fame through his marriage to the best-selling novelist Daphne du Maurier.

Not everyone was as enamored of the plan as Montgomery. U.S. Major General James Gavin, the experienced commander of the 82nd Airborne, said it looked "very rough," and de Guingand, on sick leave in England, warned from his sickbed that it was too late to launch such an operation, due to the possibility that the Germans had reinforced the area to be attacked. Rumor had it that even Browning was of two minds and warned Montgomery that Arnhem might be "a bridge too far"—the title that was eventually given to the history of the operation written by Cornelius Ryan. (It was also was made into an equally celebrated 1977 film of the same title.)

It is now clear that from the outset, Operation Market-Garden contained several flaws and that these were known to the planners. There had never been an Allied airborne operation of this size before, and weather conditions in the Low Countries in September were uncertain. But the greatest hazards were on the ground. Everything depended on the tanks of XXX Corps relieving the airborne forces and reaching Arnhem within 48 hours. This would have posed difficulties under any circumstances, but in the Netherlands, the terrain was detrimental to speed. Wooded and traversed by dykes and waterways, the countryside was unsuited to tank operations, so the armored formations would have to advance along a single road. Also, by attacking on so narrow a front, XXX Corps would pass the tactical advantage to the defenders, and the time frame was perilously tight if the Germans were to respond with artillery against the lightly armed airborne troops.

In the grim inevitability of an operation that was hastily planned and contained too many potential hazards, the assault on the Dutch bridges ran into problems almost immediately. Although the British and U.S. airborne forces completed their first drops as planned on September 17, there was a steady accumulation of delays holding up XXX Corps. There was also unexpected German resistance. Unknown to the Allies, two SS panzer divisions (the 9th and 10th) were refitting in the area and were equipped with Mark IV tanks and assorted support weapons—and happened to be training to repel a landing by airborne forces. Finally, the Germans had also come into possession of the battle plans, which had been improperly secured by the Allied officer carrying them. By the end of the first day, Model knew exactly what his opponents were going to do—and he also knew what he had to do: slow down the advance of XXX Corps and destroy the airborne forces on the ground. Those first hours decided the outcome of Market-Garden.

First to arrive on Sunday, September 17, were the glider-borne and parachute troops of the British 1st Airborne Division, and although initial casualties were light, it soon became apparent that they were facing formidable opposition in the Arnhem perimeter. They had also been dropped seven miles from the objective, and to complicate matters, their radio network promptly stopped working. The U.S. 101st Airborne Division enjoyed better fortune, landing successfully, and while the Germans managed to blow up the bridge over the Wilhelmina Canal at Zon, south of Eindhoven, the division still managed to secure its prearranged 15-mile-long corridor. To the north, the U.S. 82nd Airborne Division achieved all its initial objectives in the Grave-Groesbeek perimeter, but the Americans were frustrated at Nijmegen, where a German armored reconnaissance regiment was safeguarding the vital bridge. There were similar problems at Arnhem. Only one battalion (the 2nd Parachute Regiment) of the British airborne forces was able to seize the northern end of the road bridge but was quickly pinned down by heavy German firepower.

On the second day, all three divisions prepared to face the inevitable German counterattack. Reinforcements arrived through a second lift, but even at that early stage, the advantage passed to the German defenders as the Allied failures began to mount. The crucial bridge at Nijmegen remained in German hands, and at Arnhem, the British forces failed to create and protect a corridor between their dropping zones and the town. Discrepancies in arms and equipment also began to tell: the lightly armed airborne forces were no match for the armor and artillery ranged against them, and they soon became embroiled in a bloody fight for their own survival. This made it even more essential that the ground forces break through to relieve the steadily shrinking perimeters held by the airborne forces.

It was not to be. Although XXX Corps made some progress, its lead formation, the Guards Armoured Division, quickly got pinned down by concentrated German opposition, and all momentum was lost. By the end of the first day it had only advanced seven miles, whereas Montgomery's plans had specified a linking up with U.S. 101st Airborne Division at Eindhoven. Further delays, however, allowed the engineers to replace the blown bridge at Zon. Bad weather hampered the deployment of reinforcements from the air and also curtailed close support strikes, and it was not until September 20 that the Guards met the 82nd Airborne at Nijmegen, where the Waal River was eventually crossed using assault boats. The following day, around 1,000 men of the Polish Independent Parachute Brigade dropped at Driel, south of the Lower Rhine, to reinforce the British 1st Airborne Division in the perimeter, but they were unable to effect a river crossing. What was needed now was a determined push by XXX Corps, but this failed to materialize, and as a result the fate of the 1st Airborne was sealed.

On the night of September 25, under conditions of great secrecy, the survivors withdrew from the perimeter and made the difficult Lower Rhine crossing as Operation Market-Garden was finally wound down. Of the 11,920 British and Polish airborne soldiers who had gone into battle a week earlier, 3,910 made good on their escape; 1,485 were killed or died later of their wounds; and the rest went into German captivity. Of the U.S. forces, the 82nd Airborne Division lost 1,432 men, either killed, wounded, or missing; while the casualties in the 101st Airborne Division were 2,118 killed, wounded, or missing. Ground force casualties were equally high: XXX Corps lost 1,480 men, and its supporting VIII and XII Corps lost 3,784 between them. In the air, the Allies lost 474 crewmen and dispatchers, the majority from the Royal Air Force. It was a heavy death toll in return for possession of an unwanted holding and the failure to create a bridgehead on the Lower Rhine.

❖

The Germans saw it somewhat differently. Following their defeat in Normandy, the staving off of Market-Garden was a much-needed boost, and it also ensured that the war would continue into the following year.

In the cold arithmetic of warfare, the casualty list in return for ground gained speaks of failure or a heroic defeat at best. That is certainly the way in which the "Epic of Arnhem" and the associated actions at Eindhoven and Nijmegen came to be viewed, but at the time Operation Market-Garden seemed to be worth the risks. The Germans had been defeated in France and driven back to their frontier. They seemed to be on the point of defeat, and the Allies possessed a large and unused asset in the airborne army, which could have produced a coup de main capable of ending the war in 1944. It is little wonder that the operation produced so many historical imponderables. If it had succeeded, the Allied armies could have entered the north German plain and put themselves within striking distance of Berlin. Not only would the war have ended earlier, but the whole shape of modern Europe would have been changed and post-1945 history would have been very different.

But that did not happen, and someone had to bear the responsibility for the outcome. With the passing of the years, it is possible to see where the mistakes were made at strategic and operational levels. It was wrong to drop the forces so far from their intended targets, and equally erroneous not to fly two lifts on the first day. Once on the ground at Arnhem, the British 1st Airborne Division was sluggish in getting to its target. Faulty or inaccurate intelligence gave insufficient information about the opposition, especially the presence of the two panzer divisions. Lieutenant-General Browning failed to give the U.S. 82nd Airborne Division priority at Nijmegen, and the ground forces showed a woeful lack of initiative. Horrocks's XXX Corps had been ordered by Montgomery to ensure that the attack was "rapid and violent, without regard to what is happening on the flanks," but this did not happen.[10]

The blame must also be shared by those who planned and sanctioned the operation. As the supreme command, Eisenhower was partly culpable, if only because he endorsed a high-risk plan. But in terms of the strategic position in September 1944, when it seemed that a bold push might end the war, Eisenhower's decision was based on solid reasoning and cannot be faulted: to gain a Rhine crossing, to make use of the First Allied Airborne Army, and to destroy the V-2 launch sites in the Netherlands. As the British *Official History* ruefully put it: "Operation Market-Garden accomplished much of what it had been designed to accomplish. Nevertheless, by the merciless logic of war, Market-Garden was a failure."[11]

However, full responsibility lies with Montgomery, who should have concentrated his forces on the far less glamorous task of clearing the approaches to the port of Antwerp. For a commander who had built his reputation on caution and the application of overwhelming force to save lives, Montgomery's wholehearted enthusiasm for

Market-Garden is puzzling. He was gambling everything on the ability of the airborne forces to capture the bridges, and then on his ground forces to race forward to relieve them within an exceptionally tight timetable. In fairness to Montgomery, his optimism has to be seen within the context of the period when the operation was being planned. In the general euphoria following the Normandy breakout, there was a widespread feeling that the Germans had been broken, and this encouraged the feeling that the end of the war might be at hand. Even Montgomery succumbed to the belief, telling Brooke on the day of the operation that he was confident in getting his ground forces to Arnhem within 24 hours and would then be in a position to advance into the Ruhr. His enthusiasm was intensified by his determination to prove Eisenhower wrong by pushing his forces along a narrow front toward the Rhine. In that sense, the two men's rivalry also played a part in Montgomery's decision making at Arnhem.

CHAPTER ELEVEN

A Falling Out in the Ardennes

IN THE AFTERMATH OF THE ARNHEM DEBACLE, GENERAL CARL
Spaatz, the commander of U.S. air forces in Europe, showed
that there was no slackening in the animosity between Allied
commanders when he wrote to a friend claiming that "any
deficiency in the operation was probably more the fault of the
famous British General Montgomery than any other cause."[1]

From an American point of view, it was probably a fair,
if unnecessary, comment. Montgomery had irritated his U.S.
colleagues with his insistence on the superiority of a concentrated northern thrust, and after the Normandy landings,
there were growing doubts about the reality behind his reputation as an all-conquering battlefield general. General Omar
Bradley, in particular, was beginning to feel aggrieved about
Montgomery's "unconscionable strategic demands" and let

it be known that he would not stand idle while "that self-important SOB was allowed to win the war on his own."[2] Market-Garden's lack of success—the structural failings of the airborne plan and the absence of urgency in the ground operation—only seemed to confirm that Montgomery's star was on the wane. Not surprisingly, the Arnhem operation was the last occasion that Supreme Commander Dwight Eisenhower would accept a strategic plan from his British subordinate.

Not that any of this encouraged Montgomery to rethink his philosophy. On the contrary, he returned to the single-thrust argument with a vigor and tenacity that did not reflect Britain's new position as the junior partner in the alliance. He also began insisting once more that there had to be a unified command for all operations north of the Ardennes. At the same time, he continued to be lackadaisical about operations to secure the Scheldt River, and it took Chief of the Imperial General Staff Alan Brooke's intervention at a commanders' conference on October 5 to force him take immediate steps to grip the battle. Brooke was the one man whom Montgomery would heed, and the CIGS's diary entry for that day makes it clear that a stinging rebuke had been issued:

> During the whole discussion one fact stood out clearly, that Antwerp must be captured with the least possible delay. I feel that Monty's strategy for once is at fault, instead of carrying out the advance on Arnhem he ought to have made certain of Antwerp in the first place. [Admiral Betram] Ramsay brought this out well in discussion and criticised Monty freely.[3]

Montgomery took the hint and immediately offered encouragement to the Canadian Corps in its efforts to clear the Scheldt. Reinforcements arrived in the shape of the 7th Armoured Division, the 51st and 52nd Divisions, and the U.S. 104th Infantry Division, but at the same time he refused to relinquish his demand for the creation of a single commander for a thrust into the Ruhr. On October

10, 1944, he wrote to Eisenhower demanding that as the alliance's supreme commander, he should either run the battle himself or he should appoint Montgomery or Bradley to do it for him. This brought an immediate and furious response. "The real issue at hand," wrote Eisenhower, was Antwerp, and only when it had been secured would an assault be made on the Ruhr. Furthermore, Eisenhower continued, when it was made it would be under the direction of Bradley's 12th Army Group. If Montgomery found that solution "unsatisfactory," then it would become "our duty to refer the matter to a higher authority for any action they may chose to take, however drastic."[4] The threat of political involvement drew an unexpected riposte from Montgomery in a cable written on October 16.

> Dear Ike,
>
> I have received your letter of 13 October. You will hear no more on the subject of command from me. I have given my views and you have given your answer. That ends the matter and I and all of us up here will weigh in one hundred per cent to do what you want and we will pull it through without a doubt. I have given ANTWERP top priority in all operations in 21 Army Group and all energies and efforts will be now devoted toward opening that place.
>
> Your very devoted and loyal subordinate MONTY.[5]

However, despite Montgomery's apology, it was not the end of the matter. In November, a fresh offensive was made along a broad front, with the U.S. First and Ninth Armies attacking toward the Roer River, while General George Patton's Third Army advanced toward the Saar. As Montgomery had predicted, the attack stalled, especially in the Hürtgen Forest, where two U.S. divisions, the 4th and 8th, suffered high casualties. The weather was wet and cold, adding to the general misery and creating a high percentage of noncombat casualties. Further south, Patton's forces managed to cross the Moselle River, but Bradley was forced to admit his "plan to smash through to the Rhine and encircle the Ruhr had failed.... We were mired in a ghastly war of attrition."[6]

The situation appalled Montgomery, who noted that "the thrust was not sufficiently concentrated, nor were there sufficient reserves of fresh troops or of ammunition to maintain the offensive until a break-through had been achieved." This was undoubtedly true. The weight of the U.S. attack had been insufficient to master the difficulties of the ter-rain, and Bradley had also underestimated the fighting qualities of the opposition. With the Allied advance seeming to have come to a stand-still, Montgomery returned once more to the problems of command and control— the best analogy would be "as a dog to a bone." Although he respected Eisenhower personally, he now had grave doubts about his capacity to command armies in the field, and on November 17, he warned Brooke that "if we go drifting along as at present, we are merely playing into enemy hands, and the war will go on indefinitely."[7]

Matters came to a head once more on December 7, when Eisenhower convened a commanders' conference at Maastricht. The main item on the agenda was the reworking of Bradley's plan to strike at Germany north and south of the Ardennes, with one prong aimed at the Ruhr and the other at Frankfurt, then onward to Kassel. Once more, Montgomery argued that any splitting of Allied resources would weaken the proposed attack, and he reiterated his belief in a concerted assault on the Ruhr by up to 50 divisions. This smacked of megalo-mania and tunnel vision to the Americans, and Eisenhower would not budge on this point. In his notes for the meeting, Bradley claimed that not only did Montgomery give a poor performance, but he "refused to admit that there was any merit on anybody else's views except his own."[8] This is not an unfair observation, as Montgomery often appeared annoyingly arrogant to his U.S. colleagues, but the British field marshal was unconvinced by the proposal before him and doubted that Bradley had the necessary "giant steamroller" to smash the German defenses.

It was at this stage of the battle, when conditions were at their worst, that the Germans decided to counterattack in the Ardennes.

The plan was the brainchild of Adolf Hitler, who had reasoned as early as September that the winter weather—"night, fog, and snow"—would give the Germans the opportunity to hit the Allies back through the dense Ardennes forest, with its narrow, steep valleys, and then turn rapidly north to recapture Brussels and Antwerp. The attack would split the Allies, leaving the U.S. armies unable to come to the aid of Montgomery's 21st Army Group, which could be encircled and destroyed before it could attack the Ruhr. This was known as "Operation *Wacht am Rhein*" ("The Watch on the Rhine," also the title of a German patriotic song; it was through the Ardennes and the Eifel mountain range that Hitler had launched his blitzkrieg on France in May 1940). Despite the misgivings of the senior German generals, who wanted to limit the operation to smaller offensives aimed at disrupting the Allies, Hitler was adamant that his solution would break the Allied line and buy him valuable time to use the new V-weapons to greater effect in bombarding targets in England. In a long and rambling speech to senior commanders before the attack began, Hitler argued that a successful assault would not only divide the Allies physically but would cause political divisions that would weaken the alliance.

To fulfill the aims of Operation *Herbstnebel* ("Autumn Mist" as Wacht am Rhein was renamed), Hitler ordered the deployment of two panzer armies commanded by two of his best younger tank generals, Hasso von Manteuffel and Josef "Sepp" Dietrich, both veterans of the eastern front. To the north of the Ardennes offensive, the Sixth SS Panzer Army (Dietrich's) would attack toward the Meuse River between Huy and Liège before pushing north through Belgium toward Antwerp. Wheeling around from the west between Dinant and Namur would be the Fifth Panzer Army (von Manteuffel's) which would also cut off any attempt by the Americans to close the gap in the Allied line. A third offensive toward Luxembourg would be made by Lieutenant-General Erich Brandenberger's Seventh Infantry Army to shield the southern flank. Between them, the three armies consisted of 30 armored, Panzergrenadier, and airborne divisions, most of which had fought in

Normandy, and they had air support from 1,000 strike and fighter aircraft of Luftwaffe's Second Fighter Corps.

However, despite their strength on paper, the forces available to Dietrich and von Manteuffel had serious deficiencies. Most of the ten armored divisions had been refitted with Mark V Panther and Mark VI Tiger tanks, but gaps in personnel had been plugged by inexperienced soldiers, most of whom had not yet seen action—a motley collection of reservists, *volksgrenadiers* (ethnic Germans from eastern and central Europe), and others culled from headquarters' staffs. The average age of the soldiers in the SS panzer divisions was 18. Logistics were also a problem: just as the Allies had found themselves overstretched following the D-Day landings in Normandy, so too did the German army commanders worry that there would be insufficient fuel to take their armored divisions as far as Antwerp.

In fact, the attack got off to a good start when it began on the morning of December 16. Only four U.S. divisions of VIII Corps held the 90 miles of line in the Ardennes, and they were ill-suited to meet the concentrated German assault—one of them, the 106th Division, had not even been in combat, while the other three were recuperating from the fighting in the Hürtgen Forest. Tight security had masked the German buildup, and although the Allies had received detailed intelligence about the redeployment of key armored divisions, they believed it was for defensive purposes. (A U.S. intelligence appreciation on December 15 warned that while forces were building up behind the West Wall, this was in preparation for a "limited scale offensive...for the purpose of achieving a Christmas 'morale victory' for civilian consumption.") Even the commanders were relaxed. Bradley dismissed the idea of any immediate German attack, while Montgomery was confident enough of the strength of the Allied position to state on December 15 that "the enemy is at present fighting a defensive campaign on all fronts; his situation is such that he cannot stage major offensive operations." When the German assault began in the early morning hours the next day, planners at Eisenhower's headquarters dismissed it as "a spoiling attack" designed to test a weakly defended front.[9]

The attack, however, took U.S. Lieutenant General Courtney Hodges, responsible for the area, by surprise. Under cover of an enormous artillery bombardment, 14 German infantry divisions began their advance, backed by five panzer divisions ready to exploit the expected breakthrough. Despite the speed and aggression of the assault, geography was against the Germans, and they did well to push ahead so far and so quickly in the opening hours. The roads in the Ardennes were narrow and twisting, and the terrain, with heavily wooded slopes and deep ravines, was not suited to rapid armored assaults—hence the use of infantry to spearhead the initial phase of the battle. Strung out along the front, the U.S. divisions fought bravely, but by the end of the first day, the leading elements of the Sixth SS Panzer Army had penetrated 20 miles into Allied territory. At the same time von Manteuffel's Fifth Panzer Army was making good progress westward through the Schnee Eifel on the way to the key objectives of Bastogne and St. Vith, which controlled the main local roads. The aggression and unexpectedness of the attack caused consternation among the Allied soldiers, who believed Germany incapable of mounting offensive operations. Additionally, communications along the Allied lines broke down, and some U.S. formations panicked and retreated in the face of the attack, adding to the confusion.

In the first stages, commanders at Bradley's headquarters in Luxembourg were at a loss as to how to deal with the unexpected incursion into their front. Telephone lines had been destroyed during the opening artillery barrage, and the first indication was that the Germans were mounting a local operation aimed at containing Patton's planned attack on the Saar. However, Eisenhower was less convinced by that reasoning and showed considerable intuition by moving two divisions to reinforce the embattled front line. Three days after the attack began, Eisenhower met his senior commanders in the old French barracks at Verdun, and it was in that uninspiring setting that Patton made a decisive contribution to turning the tide of a battle which would be known to history as the Battle of the Bulge. The description was Churchill's and it referred to the bulge, 40 miles wide and 60 miles deep, created by the advancing Germans.

The conference opened with a strained and tense atmosphere. Eisenhower made little secret of the seriousness of the situation. The German attack had to be contained at all costs, and the one person who could aid the beleaguered forces in the center was Patton, who had contingency plans to move the U.S. Third Army to relieve the strategically important towns of Bastogne, St. Vith, and Houffalize. The scene was set for what would become one of the best-executed maneuvers of the campaign in Europe, as the Third Army swung into the southern flank of the bulge, a move along a 25-mile front that was executed over unfamiliar territory and along icy winter roads.

By December 22, Patton's relief force was in position and ready to move toward Bastogne, occupied by the U.S. 101st Airborne Division, which was under an increasingly desperate siege by forces from General Heinrich von Lüttwitz's 47th Panzer Corps. The following day, Patton's soldiers were in sight of the beleaguered town, but the first armored column met stout resistance when it arrived within five miles of the perimeter on the road from Arlon. However, with the weather improving, airdrops were made to aid the garrison inside Bastogne, and on Christmas Day, with German forces stalled to the north and checked short of the Meuse, von Manteuffel ordered a last attack before Patton's forces arrived. Throughout the day the U.S. defenders faced a major German assault. The defensive perimeter was breached by an armored column before being engaged by tank destroyers on the flanks, and the offensive petered out. It was not until the following day, Boxing Day, that a task force from the U.S. 4th Armored Division eventually broke through the perimeter to create a corridor into the beleaguered town.

By then, the main thrust of the German attack had been checked, and Field Marshal von Rundstedt asked Hitler for permission to consolidate his position. His request was refused, as it would signify the collapse of the original plan. Of the two German armies, von Manteuffel's had made the most ground, its leading panzer divisions bypassing Bastogne to push on toward the Meuse, but its attack had faltered when Dietrich refused to commit his mechanized infantry reserves in support of the faster-moving Fifth Panzer Army, a move that transferred the center of gravity of the German attack. It was a double mistake, as by then the Sixth SS Panzer Army had become bogged down, and its leading units were running low on fuel well short of the river. With the weather improving, the Allies were able to use their aircraft to strike the German columns at will, flying more than 15,000 sorties in the first four days of clear weather.

By then, too, Montgomery had taken over the direction of the northern sector of the battle (as of December 20), a move that gave him command of the U.S. First and Ninth Armies, which joined the battle with British XXX Corps already deployed as a mobile reserve on the west bank of the Meuse. In the initial stages of the German thrust, Montgomery had complained to Brooke that "we may now have to pay the price for the policy of drift and lack of proper control on operations which has been a marked feature of the last three months."[10] While there is some self-satisfaction in this signal, it is also true that there had been indecision in the higher U.S. headquarters and that some U.S. combat units had not performed well on the ground. Montgomery was right to point out that there was an immediate need to regain control of the battle, just as Eisenhower was right to place Hodges's forces under British control. It would have been easy to sideline Montgomery, who was by then the object of considerable dislike amongst U.S. commanders, especially Bradley; but Eisenhower was correct to make this move in a time of crisis.

In return, Montgomery repaid the confidence shown in him by realigning British and U.S. forces to create a solid defensive line on the Allied northern flank. Horrocks's XXX Corps was deployed between Liège and Louvain to block the approaches to the bridges over the Meuse, while the two U.S. armies moved into new defensive positions to blunt von Manteuffel's assault. The aim was simple: to wear out the attacking German formations against a solid wall formed by British XXX Corps and U.S. VII Corps.

Above all, however, Montgomery restored a sense of cohesion to the northern flank, and his confidence was infectious. Even skeptical U.S. forces recognized that Montgomery was in his element in taking over command of a muddled situation. One divisional commander noted that Montgomery was "a guy who really knows what he is doing," and after the war von Manteuffel admitted that the British field marshal had "turned a series of isolated actions into a coherent battle fought according to a clear and definite plan."[11] This was the correct tactical response, and Montgomery recognized the need to grip the battle, just as he had done when he took over command of the Eighth Army in North Africa. It worked, too, and together with Patton's stunning redeployment of the U.S. Third Army to the south, this was a crucial moment in the battle. The relief of Bastogne did not mark the end of the Battle of the Bulge, but it was the beginning of the end. The German attack had stalled, and the reserves had been committed, but they had still not achieved a breakthrough that would allow them to widen and deepen their front.

In early January, at the beginning of 1945, the U.S. First Army and British XXX Corps began their counterattack in the direction of Houffalize. Throughout this final fortnight of the battle, they faced fierce resistance from the German forces, who now realized that they were fighting not to reach the Meuse but to defend their retreat back into their homeland. For the German soldiers, though, the failure of the Ardennes offensive was the beginning of the decline of their defense of the western frontier. A British historian of the battle, Peter Elstob, also fought in it as a tank commander, and he could sense the new feelings of self-confidence coursing through the Allied armies.

> Now as their units were being re-equipped and brought up to strength and they looked at the unfamiliar faces of the new men steeling themselves for their first battle and they heard the almost continual sound of the big guns mercilessly shelling the Germans and saw the planes confidently dominating the sky they realised that, after all, it was going to be all right. The Germans were going to be defeated and not in their Ardennes adventure but in their whole mad attempt to dominate the world.[12]

By the end of the battle the Germans were back where they started, and Hitler's great gamble had failed. They had lost decisively, with 130,000 battlefield casualties and the destruction of more than 600 tanks and armored vehicles, as well as over 1,000 irreplaceable combat aircraft. They had held up the Allied thrust toward the Ruhr and the Saar, but only temporarily, and in so doing had left the Allies with 50,000 casualties. Hitler's hoped-for breach in the Allied command structure had failed to materialize, but at the very moment that the Germans seemed to have shot their bolt, a new and potentially disastrous rift appeared at Eisenhower's headquarters.

The already strained relations between Montgomery and his U.S. colleagues were exacerbated when the British field marshal held a press conference on January 7, 1945, in which his command of the two U.S. armies was made public. On paper, Montgomery's official statement was innocuous enough—he went out of his way to praise the fighting quality of the American soldiers and Eisenhower's leadership—but his presentation to British reporters gave the impression that he was taking the credit for winning the battle. Unfortunately, the British press seized on this line, which seemed to imply that Montgomery had saved the Americans from disaster, and when the story became public, it caused an uproar in the U.S. Army.

For the cause of Allied unity, it was a disastrous performance. Coming on top of an earlier incident on Christmas Day 1944, when

Montgomery had humiliated Bradley during a meeting at his tactical headquarters and renewed appeals to Eisenhower for a change in the command structure, it only widened the existing rift between the two armies. Instead of underlining the Allies' solidarity, the press conference simply disgusted all Americans who read the reports. A worried Eisenhower, who showed great patience throughout, admitted later that "this incident caused me more distress and worry than did any similar one of the war,"[13] and for a while relations between the two Allies hit rock bottom. Particularly exercised was Bradley: because he had been forced to watch Montgomery commanding U.S. forces, the press conference seemed to him a double insult. Not only had he been sidelined when Eisenhower thought that he had lost control of the battle, he then had to listen to the implication that Montgomery alone had saved the U.S. Army from defeat by dint of his superior leadership.

In the aftermath and in the years that followed the war, Montgomery faced deserved criticism for his performance at the press conference. The initial favorable impressions in the American press were quickly forgotten, as was Montgomery's contribution to the winning of the battle—not only had his armored formations prevented the Germans from crossing the Meuse, his attack toward Houffalize had taken some of the pressure off Patton. Although these tactics were by their nature limited, and Montgomery was later criticized for a lack of aggression in mounting a major counterattack, at the time it was the correct way to handle a battle that had been slipping away from the Allies. It was not a brilliant victory; it was unglamorous and painstaking, but it was effective. For that Montgomery deserves full credit. The tragedy is that he allowed this triumph to go to his head by pressing Eisenhower with his long-running argument to be given overall command of the Allied ground forces for the final push into Germany.

CHAPTER TWELVE

Crossing the Rhine

BY THE END OF 1944, THE SUMMER BLITZKRIEG DASH OUT OF NORMANDY was but a warm memory for the Allied armies as they faced the increasingly bitter winter conditions of northwest Europe. By then, too, the war of movement had given way to a war of attrition across the long front from the English Channel to the Swiss border, and it was taking its toll on men and equipment. At that stage in the campaign, the Allies' supreme commander, General Dwight Eisenhower, had at his disposal 73 divisions, the majority of which were American (49 U.S., 12 British, 8 French, 3 Canadian, and 1 Polish), and he planned to use this overwhelming strength to advance steadily and methodically into Germany. Ahead lay the obstacle of the Rhine. Eisenhower decided to address it on a broad front, using Montgomery's 21st Army Group and the U.S. Ninth Army to make a pincer movement to the north that would roll up the German Army Group B, while U.S. General Omar

Bradley's forces would advance toward the Rhine between Cologne and Koblenz. At a chiefs of staff planning conference held in Malta on January 29 and 30, the main thrust of the plans, under the codenames "Veritable" and "Grenade," was agreed as follows:

> Phase I: Montgomery was to seize the west bank of the Rhine from Nijmegen to Düsseldorf, after clearing the Lower Rhineland with converging attacks—from the Reichswald by First Canadian Army and from the Roer River by the U.S. Ninth Army, which was to remain under his command for the Rhine crossing. During these operations, apart from capturing the Roer dams and covering Ninth Army's southern flank, Bradley's forces on the Ardennes front were to maintain an aggressive defence.

> Phase II: While Montgomery was preparing for a set-piece assault across the Lower Rhine, Bradley was to secure the west bank from Düsseldorf to Koblenz. For this purpose First Army was to drive its left wing through to Cologne and then strike south-east into the flank and rear of the Germans in the Eifel, whereupon Third Army was to take up the offensive, attacking eastwards from Prüm to Koblenz.

> Phase III: While Montgomery was assaulting the Lower Rhine, the Third and Seventh American Armies were to clear out the Moselle-Saar-Rhine triangle and secure crossing places on the Mainz-Karlsruhe sector for the forces which were to carry out the southern envelopment of the Ruhr.[1]

From the shape of the plans, it was clear that the lion's share of the battle and the bulk of the Allies' assets would be given to Montgomery in the northern sector, while once again the U.S. forces had been relegated to guarding the flanks. Characteristically, Bradley bridled at the proposals, which seemed to deny him a major role in the final triumph—the successful invasion of Germany and the capture of its capital, Berlin. In turn, Bradley proposed that the main thrust into Germany should made through the center, with the four U.S. armies driving through the Ardennes toward the Cologne-Koblenz sector while Montgomery guarded the northern flank and the First French

Army protected the southern flank between Strasbourg and the Swiss border. To the immense chagrin of the U.S. generals, Eisenhower rejected Bradley's plan, and at the beginning of February 1945, Montgomery was given the green light to push ahead with Phase I, the main assault on the Rhine and Ruhr using the First Canadian Army, the Second British Army, and the U.S. Ninth Army.

Operation Veritable began on February 8 with five infantry divisions backed by three armored brigades advancing along an eight-mile front from Nijmegen, with the Rhine on their left and the Maas to their right. It was a typical Montgomery set-piece battle: before the assault, there was a huge artillery barrage involving 1,034 guns that lasted five hours—the heaviest of its kind seen in the war. Although the bombardment caused panic among the German defenders, many of whom were reservists or medically downgraded men, the initial attack faltered when the advancing units ran into areas that had been deliberately flooded. The Germans' deployment of their First Parachute Army also caused difficulties, and the British and Canadian forces were soon embroiled in a desperate battle in the Reichswald, a heavily forested area with only two north-south routes (Kranenburg to Hekkens and Kleve to Goch, along the eastern edge) and no readily usable east-west route.

The Germans had created three defensive lines. The first was manned by the 84th Division and the 1st Parachute Regiment and ran from Wyler to the Maas along the western edge of the Reichswald; the second lay beyond the forest and was centered on the towns of Rees, Kleve, and Goch; while the third ran from Rees to Geldern. All the enemy strongpoints mounted dogged resistance, and their cause was helped by the waterlogged terrain, which meant that Allied progress depended on the ability of a fully loaded infantry soldier to move through mud and water while under enemy fire. By February 11, the 15th (Scottish) Division and 43rd Infantry Division had pushed through Kleve, but it took a whole week to advance a further five miles. Goch proved to be a particularly difficult target surrounded by antitank ditches and fortified strongpoints, and it was not until February 18 that the 15th (Scottish) Division, supported by brigades from the 51st (Highland) and 53rd (Welsh) Divisions, was able to fight its way into the fortified town. Some idea of the problems facing the attacking infantrymen can be gleaned from the war diaries of the infantry battalions involved in the operation. As the 7th/9th Royal Scots approached Goch, it was thought to be lightly defended, but that perception was quickly altered when the Germans responded with heavy mortar and machine-gun fire. It took three more days to take the northern part of Goch, and there was "some tough fighting before those resolute enemy troops were ejected from the town."[2] In the days that followed, the same battalion was engaged in equally hard fighting on the high ground overlooking Schloss Kalbeck.

Having secured the bulk of the Reichswald, Montgomery ordered the second part of his pincer operation to be launched on February 23. Code-named "Grenade," this involved the U.S. First and Ninth Armies attacking northeastward to the Rhine between Düsseldorf and Wesel. Again it was a hard-pounding battle fought over terrain made even more treacherous by flooding, in this case thanks to the German decision to blow up the dams on the Roer River, and it was not until March 3 that the U.S. forces made contact with the British and Canadians. During the fighting the Allies had 15,500 casualties killed, wounded, or missing; but even though the Germans fought with grim determination, they had had lost their last formal battle of the war. On March 9, the First Parachute Army abandoned the Wesel pocket and withdrew across the Rhine.

Operations Veritable and Grenade had both been planned meticulously by Montgomery, and both had achieved his objective of cracking open the German defenses by using concentrated artillery fire and by deploying infantry in large numbers during the assault phase. In his history of the British Army during the Second World War, General Sir David Fraser, who fought in the battle as a junior officer with the Grenadier Guards, remembered that every position was won with great difficulty due to the rigors of the terrain and the ferocity displayed by the defenders:

> It had been as hard fighting as any phase of the North-West European campaign, fought in the inhospitable winter of the lower Rhineland, on a narrow front where the only tactic was to apply massed artillery fire and batter at a stoutly defended door. It could not be assisted by mobility or manoeuvre. [Operation] Veritable was a killing match; slow, deadly and predictable. It was the last of its kind.[3]

Fraser could have added that it was the ideal fight for a commander like Montgomery. The Reichswald battle was neither glamorous nor subtle, and the outcome depended on the determination of the soldiers, but in the end, it was successful. Several British participants referred to it at the time as "a typical Monty setup," with a massive concentration of artillery along a narrow front and the imposition of overwhelming force to grind down determined opposition. It was also a masterly prelude to the next stage: the crossing of the Rhine, Germany's last frontier and the key to victory.

The eventual capture of Goch followed by the fall of another German strongpoint at Hekkens allowed Montgomery to fine-tune his plans for the Rhine crossing. But at this crucial stage, inter-Allied rivalry once again intruded on Eisenhower's plans for the eastward advance. Both Bradley and General George Patton were determined that U.S. forces were the first to cross the Rhine, and in this aim they were partially successful. On March 7, forward units of the U.S. First Army captured the intact bridge at Remagen, and two weeks later, Patton's Third Army started crossing the Rhine in boats at Oppenheim. The latter operation was greeted by an exultant Bradley, who was still smarting about the decision to give prominence to the British and Canadian assault in the north, but the news was met with equanimity at Montgomery's headquarters. On receiving Bradley's triumphant signal that Patton had crossed the Rhine "without the benefit of aerial bombardments, ground smoke, artillery preparation and airborne assistance" Montgomery told Eisenhower that it was "an excellent move as it would be an unpleasant threat to the enemy and would undoubtedly draw enemy strength on it and away from my business in the north."[4]

Besides, the *schwerpunkt* of the battle for the Rhine still lay to the north. Whatever else had happened at Oppenheim, where the Rhine was only half as wide as it was at Wesel, the key to the north German plain and the defeat of Germany in the west lay in Montgomery's area of operations across the lower Rhine. The plans were drawn up accordingly. Montgomery planned to move across the Rhine along a 12-mile front using the same forces that had brought him success in the Reichswald and the Roer. On the right flank, XII Corps (led by Lieutenant-General Neil Ritchie) would attack with four divisions—the 7th Armoured, the 15th, 52nd, and 53rd—with backup from four independent brigades and supporting artillery. On the left, Horrocks's XXX Corps had five divisions—the Guards Armoured, 3rd Infantry, 43rd Infantry, 51st (Highland), and 3rd Canadian with supporting artillery. To the south, Lieutenant General W. H. Simpson's U.S. Ninth Army would cross between Duisburg and Wesel, while the actual crossing would be reinforced by two airborne divisions dropped along a five-mile front to secure the ground for the assault into Westphalia.

For the first crossing, Montgomery selected 1 Commando Brigade to make the crossing at Wesel with 15th (Scottish) Division, while the 51st (Highland) Division would cross at Rees. According to Sir Martin Lindsay, a company commander in the 1st Gordon Highlanders, "Montgomery was supposed to have said that Scottish troops were the best for assaulting."[5] Using newly developed amphibious vehicles known as Buffaloes, they began the operation on the night of March 23 and quickly proved Montgomery's confidence in them. For the 7th Argyll and Sutherland Highlanders, one of the assault battalions, this meant crossing the river at Rees, northwest of Wesel, and according to the battalion historian, "it was a thrilling moment when these great clumsy vehicles lumbered into the water and started swimming across to the far bank."[6] Once on the other side, the battalion was involved in heavy fighting to take the village of Bienen, where the opposition's resistance was intense. During the same operation, the 5th/7th Gordon Highlanders landed to the east of Rees, while the 1st Gordon Highlanders followed the 5th Black Watch in an attack that was delayed by the inability of the returning Buffaloes to climb out of the river. During the actual operation this was corrected, and a description of the crossing was later written up by a recorder in the 1st Gordons for the regimental records:

> The Buffaloes slowly crawled over the fields, then dipped into the water, became water-borne, and then one had the feeling of floating down out of control, yet each Buffalo churned without difficulty out of Germany's greatest barrier and at the right place by the flickering green light. Once aground the Buffaloes with vehicles took one 200 yards inland, those with troops deposited their load on the green fields, now baked hard by the recent fine weather, at the water's edge; two bunds [dykes], each about ten feet high, stood against the skyline; otherwise the flatness was unbroken.[7]

Despite the ferocity of the opposition, all the Scottish battalions got safely across the river, and by nightfall 15th (Scottish) Division had linked up with British 6th Airborne Division to secure the opposite bank. Within 48 hours the first bridges for heavy vehicles had been put in place, and the bridgehead was pushed forward ten miles toward the Issel River. Further south, Simpson's U.S. forces also crossed successfully, and six divisions were soon pushing toward Schermbeck. And even further to the south, Patton's forces made successful crossings between Boppard and Groer, while the U.S. Seventh Army crossed near Worms on March 26, and the French First Army completed the operation near Germersheim five days later.

Helped by good weather, the Rhine crossings had been a complete success and fully vindicated the optimism that Montgomery had brought to the planning of the operation in the north. Given the weight of the Allied attack and the lack of a German strategic reserve—their Sixth Army had been moved to the eastern front—Montgomery was in a strong position, and his personal message to the troops reflected his sense that the end of the war was nigh:

> The complete and decisive defeat of the Germans is certain; there is no possibility of doubt on this matter.
> 21 army group will now cross the Rhine.
> The enemy thinks he is safe behind this great river obstacle...but we will show the enemy that he is far from safe behind it.[8]

Even so, Montgomery also understood the capacity of the German Army to resist and continue the fight—51st (Highland) Division had lost its popular and effective commander, Major-General Tom Rennie, in a mortar attack at Rees—and everyone involved in the operation knew that it was essential to cross the Rhine quickly and effectively to create the necessary bridgehead for further operations. In the aftermath of the battle, Montgomery was accused by Bradley and others of employing excessive force for the Rhine crossing and misusing airborne forces to secure the bridgehead. (That helps to account for the praise Bradley heaped on Patton for crossing the Rhine at Oppenheim without any fanfare.) While it is true that the infantry could have taken their objectives alone, Montgomery did not want to risk lives and resources at the very moment when he wanted to push into the heart of Germany. Operation Varsity (as it was known) proved to be the most successful airborne operation of the war, and U.S. Lieutenant General Lewis Brereton described it as "a breathtaking attack without which the ground forces' task would have been many times more difficult."[9]

Once across the river, when it became clear that the defending Germans were in fact an army on the verge of defeat, Montgomery's instinct was to push ahead rapidly into the north German plain toward the Elbe River. On March 27, he informed Eisenhower that his intention was to "drive hard" toward the Elbe, with the U.S. Ninth Army targeting Magdeburg, while the British Second Army moved on the left toward Hamburg with the next objective being Berlin.

◆

It was at this stage that Eisenhower intervened decisively to change Allied plans and to deny Montgomery the opportunity to race forward in the north. On March 28, having read Montgomery's proposal, he ordered him to meet with Bradley in the Kassel-Paderborn area, where the U.S. Ninth Army was about to revert to American command for the envelopment and occupation of the Ruhr. During these operations, the British Second Army would protect Bradley's northern flank as they marched toward Dresden to join up with advancing Soviet forces. For Montgomery this was a stinging blow. Instinct told him that the opposition had been neutered and that now was the time to exploit that weakness by moving decisively into the north German plain. He was right to feel that way, and the last thing he wanted was to become involved in an envelopment operation in the Ruhr he believed would be both time-consuming and costly in casualties. But what Montgomery did not know was that other aspects, political and national, were now intruding on the western Allies' direction of the war.

Unknown to Montgomery, the Chief of the Imperial General Staff, Alan Brooke, had agreed to a fresh revision of the Allied plan by Eisenhower, who now wanted to secure the Ruhr before pushing the bulk of his forces southeast to Dresden. Although this seems a strange decision, Eisenhower had reasons he could not divulge to his army commanders, and not even Bradley was informed until later. At the end of March, Eisenhower had received a signal from Washington informing him that he had to reach an agreement with the Soviet Union about the lines of demarcation their armies would use to prevent a possible collision as the Allies advanced into Germany. Accordingly, he informed Stalin that the western Allies would not advance toward Berlin but would meet up with Soviet forces in the Erfurt-Leipzig-Dresden sector. The decision was endorsed by U.S. General George

Marshall, and not even British prime minister Winston Churchill was permitted to offer any adverse opinion, although he was furious that Berlin would now be allowed to fall into Soviet hands. Barely a week later, the situation was complicated by Roosevelt's death in office on April 12. His successor, Harry S. Truman, was not interested in reopening the argument about who should be the first to reach Berlin.

Predictably, Montgomery was enraged and bewildered by this turn of events, but at this late stage, Brooke pointedly reminded him, his views were already fully known to Eisenhower, so he "should take no further action."[10] The British 21st Army Group was an ever more junior partner in the coalition, and Eisenhower was no longer prepared to give way to the uncooperative field marshal. Suddenly Montgomery was forced to pay the penalty for his frequently insolent behavior toward Eisenhower and his constant belittling of Bradley. Besides, there were other reasons for dropping Berlin as a target. Bradley estimated that his 12th Army Group could sustain up to 100,000 casualties in any break-in battle, "a pretty stiff price for a prestige objective."[11]

While that estimate was probably over-pessimistic, no one knew at that stage how long the Germans would resist, especially while Hitler was still alive. There was also a fear that the Nazi leadership would move into the mountainous terrain of southern Bavaria and western Austria to form a kind of "national redoubt," from which they could direct their final resistance. An intelligence summary produced by Eisenhower's headquarters on March 11 predicted a dire outline of future events, with the Germans planning a last-ditch stand by creating an underground army and equipping it with modern and unspecified secret weapons. Only after the war had ended were those fears revealed as being groundless, the propagandist exaggerations of a handful of fanatical Nazis prepared to fight to the last man.

Faced by that threat, which was heightened by the resistance of the German forces in Northern Italy and the unexplained deployment of the Sixth SS Panzer Army in the Danube Valley, Eisenhower decided that the best option was to order Bradley to drive hard into central

Germany, splitting the country in half and joining up with the Soviets in the Leipzig-Dresden area. At the same time, the left flank would be taken up by Montgomery's men as they pushed toward Hamburg and the Baltic, while the right flank wheeled southeast toward the Danube. This changed the weight of the advance and left Montgomery with stretched forces to clear north Germany and move up toward the Baltic and the border with Denmark. In fact, Eisenhower's last major operational order was to direct Montgomery to abandon his flanking guard duties and to move rapidly to secure the Kiel Canal, which links the Baltic and North Seas; this time the supreme commander promised that he would "do anything at all that is possible to help you insure the speed and success of the operation."[12]

As Montgomery only had two armies at his disposal (British and Canadian), he was hard-pressed to execute the order, but on the night of April 29, in a reprise of the Rhine crossing, the Elbe was breached at Lauenburg and Artlenburg. Once across the river, the assault battalions found that the German defenders were in no mood to surrender—indeed, some units seemed to fight with a greater fanaticism as they fell back deeper into the "Fatherland." Hitler Youth battalions proved to be particularly troublesome. When the 2nd Gordon Highlanders came across an uncompromising young woman who claimed that the Nazis would never surrender until every man was killed, she received the curt response from the advancing British soldiers they were "killing off Nazi soldiers with that purpose in view."[13] By then, though, in spite of the pockets of fierce resistance the British and Canadian forces encountered, the end was not far away. On May 1, as Soviet forces fought their way toward Hitler's command bunker in Berlin, the first units of the British 11th Armoured Division entered the town of Lübeck, and Montgomery was able to report to Brooke: "Alls well that ends well and the whole of the SCHLESWIG peninsula and DENMARK is now effectively sealed off and we shall keep it so."[14]

With Hitler dead—he had committed suicide on April 30 and it was reported in the news immediately—the eventual capitulation of the German forces was now inevitable, and it was apposite that Montgomery should have been a key player in the unconditional surrender of the German forces in the north. This took place at Lüneberg Heath on May 4, when the instruments of surrender were read aloud before the German delegation. Hostilities ceased the following day. Later that evening Montgomery was persuaded to drink some champagne at dinner, but as had been his practice throughout the conflict, he retired to his caravan at his usual time and put out the light with his customary punctuality. Three days later, on May 8, the Germans' final surrender was ratified in Berlin by Field Marshal Wilhelm von Keitel.

Although Montgomery's two armies played a subsidiary role in the final weeks of the war, their movements were still essential to cornering the German forces in the north and securing both the Kiel Canal and the border with Denmark. Much of the fighting was methodical and painstaking, as the men naturally did not want to risk their lives in the final days of the war—for instance, it took four days for XII Corps to suppress German opposition in the Lüneberg sector, and it was not until April 23 that Hamburg finally fell into British hands. Lack of logistic support was another reason for the slow advance north. As Montgomery told Brooke, the absence of the U.S. Ninth Army from his order of battle prevented him from benefiting from vital engineering resources, especially during the Elbe crossing.

❖

No discussion of Montgomery's leadership during the final days of the Second World War can exclude the unique role played by his liaison officers. This select group of 40 middle-ranking officers had emerged in Normandy to act as Montgomery's "gallopers" on the battlefield. Their job was to take orders to the front line, return with assessments, and generally act as the field marshal's "eyes and ears" as the battle unfolded. Most were young, dashing, adventurous, and totally without fear: "a wild bunch," according to one of their own, Major Peter Earle. Montgomery revered them. They played a major role in running communications during operations and often took unnecessary risks or bent the rules as they went about their business. Every evening, after dinner, Montgomery would sit down with them to receive their findings and listen to what they had seen and heard. "As a result of their reports," noted Lieutenant-General Brian Horrocks, "Monty was probably the only man who had a completely up-to-date picture of the whole battlefront."[15] Churchill was equally impressed by the system, likening it to the way Wellington had used his divisional commanders during the fighting against Napoleonic France in the Iberian Peninsula between 1808 and 1814.

When one of the Liaison Officers, Major John Poston, was killed during the advance toward Bremen, Montgomery was distraught. Not only had he lost a talented staff officer, but Poston had served earlier as his aide-de-camp in Egypt, and Montgomery treated him like a son. Unlike other Allied commanders who seemed largely indifferent to the loss of life—Patton or the Soviet General Georgy Zhukov, for example—Montgomery was sensitive and often openly moved about the deaths of soldiers close to him. It was a demonstration of humanity unusual in a battlefield commander.

CHAPTER THIRTEEN

Cold War Warrior

By the end of the Second World War, Montgomery was Britain's best-known soldier, and his military reputation was at its peak. He had been part of the Allied command structure that had defeated the Nazis and their aligned armies, and it had largely been due to his planning and foresight that the campaign in Europe had been so successful in 1944 and 1945. As "Monty," he was lionized by the British press and hugely respected by the majority of the soldiers who had served under him during the war, who felt in no small measure that they owed their lives to his careful planning and attention to detail. General Sir David Fraser spoke for many when he claimed that Montgomery had "dominated the collective consciousness of the British Army" during the long years of fighting from North Africa to Northwest Europe.[1] Still instantly recognizable in his battered battle dress and black beret with two badges, Montgomery also had the knack of being able to raise spirits with well-chosen phrases when giving morale-boosting speeches or making public appearances. In short, his persona and the aura surrounding him were almost as important as what he had actually achieved during six years of war.

Of course, not everyone warmed to him or was impressed by his achievements. Quite apart from the enemies he had made among the American generals, several of his British colleagues detested him, and even Churchill was increasingly paranoid about the field marshal's popularity. In July 1945, the Labour Party won the postwar general election, and the new prime minister was Clement Attlee, who also entertained reservations about Montgomery. As a result of this disruption, there was a delay in naming Montgomery to the post of British military governor in the quadripartite control commission established to administer defeated Germany, and this appointment was not ratified until July. There was a further delay in deciding who should succeed Alan Brooke as Chief of the Imperial General Staff. At the termination of hostilities, he had announced his intention to retire from the army, but the incoming Labour government had persuaded him to remain in office until the following year. Originally, it seemed to be accepted that Field Marshal Lord Alexander would succeed Brooke, but instead he was chosen as the next governor-general of Canada, and that left Montgomery as the only credible candidate. He was made a viscount (a singular honor that gave him a seat in the House of Lords) in the summer of 1946, prior to being appointed CIGS in succession to Brooke. His colleagues were Sir Arthur Tedder (the Chief of Air Staff, Royal Air Force), who acted as chairman of the chiefs of staff committee, and Admiral of the Fleet Sir John Cunningham (First Sea Lord, Royal Navy).

During the war, under the chairmanship of Brooke, the chiefs of staff had created a sense of coherence that had been essential for winning the conflict. Through their professionalism and sense of responsibility, they had harnessed Britain's contribution to the war effort and had hammered out a working relationship with Churchill and

Parliament. The alliance with the United States had also prospered in spite of occasional misunderstandings, and there was an optimistic belief that the prestige created during the war years would be carried over into the postwar peace. However, it was not to be. Although Attlee, the new prime minister and leader of the Labour Party, had served in the war cabinet, he believed in governing by consensus—according to one contemporary political observer, he acted like "a schoolmaster, who kept order very well but did not really teach you very much."[2]

There was also a clash of personalities among the chiefs themselves, and Montgomery deserves some of the blame. For starters, he maintained his wartime dislike of Tedder, which had begun in Normandy in 1944 as a result of Montgomery discovering that the air marshal had attempted to have him fired on account of the setbacks during Operation Goodwood. He also came to detest Cunningham, believing him to be too clever for his own good. (And both, it should be said, reciprocated his disdain.) Personal jealousy also played a part. Montgomery was better known than his navy and air force counterparts, and that rankled—not least because he had such flair for personal publicity. But the main reason for the breakdown of purpose was the inability of any of the men to work in common cause. That lack of unity would color everything the chiefs of staff attempted to achieve in the difficult postwar period.

There was a great deal to be done as Britain began winding down its bloated armed forces and facing up to the challenges of the postwar world. Demobilization was administered based on a points system that took into account years of service and personal skills, but conscription was kept in place as National Service, which required every able-bodied young man to complete a period of service in the armed forces. Otherwise, British defense policy evolved with three main pillars: the defense of western Europe; the defense of maritime lines of communication; and a commitment to the Middle East, with its strategically important artery, the Suez Canal. On the operational level, too, there was a need to maintain the garrison in Palestine, where increased Zionist immigration was leading to tensions with the indigenous Arab population, and it had already become clear that Britain would not be able to hang on to India much longer.

To tackle those problems, the chiefs of staff met twice weekly, but the mutual antagonism almost destroyed the wartime cohesion so carefully nurtured by Brooke. According to historians of the chiefs of staff, Montgomery was largely to blame for this disarray: "Supremely self-confident after his wartime victories, he saw himself as a military Messiah, sent to insure that the faults of the inter-war years were not repeated for a second time."[3] As he had done so often in the past, Montgomery liked to prepare thoroughly for meetings so that he could master every problem before it was debated. The trouble was that he frequently over-simplified issues and became impatient when others failed to see his point of view. He was not a team player, becoming irritated and even dictatorial when his ideas were not accepted. It did not help that he was contemptuous of Attlee and his cabinet colleagues, accusing them of being "wet" or failing to have any workable plans. Last but not least, he caused considerable offense by using his global fame to embark on a number of high-profile and well-publicized tours to meet world leaders—trips that not only added to his popularity but also increased his conceit and self-importance.

By any standards, Montgomery's tenure as CIGS was not his finest hour, and much of his personal behavior was reprehensible. But it would be wrong to say that he was a complete failure. On the contrary, his boundless energy and tireless imagination helped to lay the foundations for the creation of the North Atlantic Treaty Organization (NATO), the western alliance that defined the postwar world. True to previous form, Montgomery operated in his own style and brooked no interference from his fellow chiefs of staff or Attlee's government. In August 1946, he decided to accept a long-standing invitation from the Canadian government to make a goodwill tour of the country and receive a number of honorary degrees from Canadian universities. This gave him an excuse to contact Dwight Eisenhower, who had been appointed army chief of staff in succession to George

Marshall, and wheedle an invitation to visit him in Washington. This was quickly forthcoming, and Montgomery crossed the Atlantic determined to sow the seeds of a transatlantic alliance to oppose what he perceived to be the growing Soviet threat in Europe.

Before he set out on his tour, Montgomery had been ordered not to discuss any material issue with Canadian or U.S. politicians, but he had every intention of doing just that. In Ottawa he met Prime Minister William Lyon Mackenzie King, who not only agreed that transatlantic military cooperation was essential, he gave him permission to speak on Canada's behalf when he met President Harry S. Truman in Washington. This led to a top-secret meeting with the U.S. chiefs of staff to discuss the possible renewal of the wartime joint council of chiefs. Engineered by Eisenhower, the discussions took place under the guise of a cruise down the Potomac on board the yacht *Sequoia* to visit George Washington's house at Mount Vernon. As a result of this day's work, a series of highly classified political and military discussions were initiated, and from these sprang the Western European Union, which came into being in 1948, followed by NATO a year later. In a signal to his deputy, General Sir Frank Simpson, Montgomery explained that both Truman and King had "expressed their wish that we should cease being merely on friendly terms, but should get down to full and frank discussions of all defence matters," and he returned to Britain believing that some positive progress had been made.[4]

Montgomery's enthusiasm, however, for the creation of a transatlantic alliance was not shared by his fellow chiefs of staff nor by the British politicians. The former disliked the notion of entering into a new coalition, as it would oblige Britain to commit ground forces to the defense of Europe, perhaps permanently, and it would also threaten the primacy of the Royal Navy's maritime strategy. Attlee was furious, mainly because he had not authorized the talks, but also because he knew that he would never be able to get any agreement from the left wing of his party for what would seem to them to be an anti-Soviet pact. If the talks had ever become public, it would have been disastrous for the government, and had the CIGS been any other commander than Montgomery, he would almost certainly have been sacked or ordered to take early retirement.

There were also wider international issues to take into account. At the beginning of 1947, Attlee dropped the bombshell that Britain would quit India by the summer of 1948. It turned out to be somewhat earlier—August 15 of that same year—but the decision placed in jeopardy the position of Palestine, which was rapidly turning into a battleground between Zionist and Arab fighters, with the British army attempting to keep the peace. Both events colored Montgomery's role as CIGS, and during the summer there was further turbulence when Attlee agreed to hand over the British mandate in Palestine to the recently formed United Nations. To Montgomery, this smacked of weakness but, damaged economically by the war years, Britain had little option but to cut back on its imperial commitments.

It came as something of a relief for all concerned when Montgomery's tenure as CIGS came to an abrupt end in September 1948. He left after being appointed chairman of the military arm of the Western European Union, which had come into being as a result of the Treaty of Brussels earlier in the year. Formed by Britain, France, Belgium, Luxembourg, and the Netherlands, the union was a mutual defense alliance that also promoted economic, cultural, and social collaboration and laid the basis for future regeneration in Europe. Montgomery would have preferred to have been styled as "supreme commander," but he had to content himself with the title of "Chairman of the Commanders-in-Chief Committee," and in that role he was soon on a collision course with the soldier appointed commander in chief of the alliance's land forces, General Jean de Lattre de Tassigny, a former commander of the French First Army and until recently inspector general of the French armed forces.

What followed was not edifying. De Lattre was opinionated, ambitious, and single-minded, and he quickly made it clear that he would not bow to the wishes of a man whom he regarded as a mere coordinator. Montgomery believed just as fervently that he should have been named the supreme commander, and suddenly the tables were turned as he received a taste of the treatment he had meted out to Eisenhower in 1944 and 1945. Throughout the stormy relationship with de Lattre, Montgomery found that he was incapable of controlling his unruly French subordinate, who was determined to get his way on all operational matters in Europe. It proved to be an unevenly matched struggle. Just as Montgomery had been unsuited to political intrigue while working in Whitehall as CIGS, so too did he discover that the European politicking was beyond his control while attempting to direct the Western European Union's armed forces. All the while, the situation in Europe was worsening following the Soviet blockade of Berlin in the summer of 1948, and it was soon clear that the western Allies would need to adopt a new posture to meet the growing confrontation with the Soviet Union and its Eastern Bloc allies.

It had also become obvious that any new alliance would require the active cooperation of the United States, and to meet that need NATO came into being on April 4, 1949. Consisting of the Western European Union nations plus the United States, Canada, Portugal, Italy, Norway, Denmark, and Iceland, NATO's role was formulated on the principle that an attack on any member would be considered an attack against them all. The new alliance was largely symbolic, but the outbreak of the war in Korea in the summer of 1950 galvanized the member states and led to the creation of a new, integrated military command structure with Eisenhower as supreme commander.

For Montgomery, this was both a challenge and an opportunity. With his usual alacrity, he set about promoting his claims for a senior post, informing Eisenhower that he was prepared to serve loyally under his command. While that had a conciliatory ring, Eisenhower had little desire to repeat the experiences of the command structure during the war, and he also had to take into account the concerns of the other European allies who wanted equal representation in the new alliance. To Montgomery, this was complicating the issue, and his solution was starkly simple: there should be separate sea, land, and air force commanders for the forces in the northern, southern, and central sectors with a deputy supreme commander reporting directly to Eisenhower. Although Eisenhower was wary of any solution that would replicate wartime problems, Montgomery's plan was broadly accepted, and on March 12, 1950, he was appointed to deputize for the supreme commander and to take over responsibility for all aspects of equipping and training national forces within NATO. Under this arrangement it was understood that Montgomery would no longer have field command (unless Eisenhower was incapacitated) but would instead author the military ethos behind the new Supreme Headquarters Allied Powers Europe (SHAPE). It was a sensible arrangement, for although Montgomery had lost none of his enthusiasm or his dedication to soldiering, he was getting older—almost 64, a time when many men of his period were considering retirement. He led an abstemious life, eschewed alcohol, ate sparingly, and retired to bed at 9:30 P.M. with the light going out half an hour later. Even so, the passing of the years was bound to take a toll.

In general, Montgomery's relationship with the supreme commander worked better than it had during the war years, but all that changed in 1952, when Eisenhower stood down after 17 months in office to run as the Republican candidate for the U.S. presidency. Relations with his successor General Matthew Ridgway were less smooth, mainly because the former U.S. Airborne commander made it clear that while he would listen to Montgomery's views, his decision on any issue would be final. In response, Montgomery schemed tirelessly against Ridgway, who only lasted in office until the summer of 1953 when he returned to Washington as army chief of staff. He was replaced by General Alfred Gruenther, with whom Montgomery forged a good working relationship until he retired from active service on September 10, 1958.

⊞

By then Montgomery was almost 72 and had spent exactly 50 years in the service of the British army. Any thoughts that he was about to bow out of public life were quickly dispelled. Given his public standing and the role he had played in the previous war, it was only to be expected that he would be invited to write his memoirs. As a serving soldier he could not do this until he retired, but as early as summer 1954 he had he had entered into an agreement with Kemsley Newspapers, publishers of the influential *Sunday Times*, for the serialization of his memoirs, which would be published by the house of William Collins. The resulting book, which was given the simple title *Memoirs*, was published in fall 1958; rights were licensed all over the world, and it quickly became an international best seller. As the author intended, it also caused a sensation and became, in the words of Montgomery's biographer Nigel Hamilton "a signal for some impassioned blood-letting."[5] Those on the receiving end of the author's criticisms were furious, while those who admired his frankness thought that it was a first-class effort. Auchinleck was particularly outraged by the assertion that he had contemplated a withdrawal from the El Alamein position before Montgomery took over command on Eighth Army. The book caused a good deal of unhappiness and might have led to legal action but for some deft peacemaking.

But the main anger was felt in the United States, where it was perceived that Montgomery had traduced Eisenhower's battlefield command and that his prevarications had caused the war to be extended by a year. To many Americans this kind of backbiting seemed disrespectful to a decorated soldier who was also their president. According to the U.S. military historian Stephen Ambrose, Eisenhower was "absolutely incensed" by what Montgomery had written about him, and so deep was the hurt that he severed contact with his erstwhile colleague and deputy.[6] It has to be said that by then Eisenhower had published his own account, *Crusade in Europe* (1948), which had contained criticisms of Montgomery and Brooke, and it would have been only human if Montgomery had taken the opportunity to gain some measure of revenge. Eisenhower had been equally outraged by some of Brooke's comments when his diaries were published by Sir Arthur

Bryant in *The Turn of the Tide* and *Triumph in the West* (1957 and 1959), and Churchill, too, had added his own singular account in his six-volume *The Second World War* (1948–1954).

The events of 1944 and 1945 became steeped in controversy—differing accounts of the breakout from Normandy and the failure to take Caen, the struggle over the broad front and the narrow thrust into Germany, and the failings in the Ardennes. All too often, the debates split along nationalistic lines, with most British historians backing Montgomery and their American counterparts arguing that many of Montgomery's claims had been falsified or based on his own interpretation of events. It is an indication of the strength of feeling on both sides that 60 years later these issues are still alive. Although in his *Memoirs* Montgomery was often guilty of refashioning episodes to show him in a good light (as was Eisenhower in his own memoirs), his account is a model of its kind and received plaudits at the time of publication for its clear and direct literary style.

In other respects, Montgomery enjoyed a reasonably tranquil retirement. Although he caused some offense for his increasingly bizarre opinions—he used his position in the House of Lords to attack the United States' war effort in Vietnam and to criticize the passing of the Sexual Offences Act in 1967, which partially decriminalized homosexual acts between consenting men over the age of 21—Montgomery in his dotage became increasingly divorced from events around him. With the onset of the 1970s, his closest friends noted a waning of his powers, and he died on March 24, 1976, at his home at Isington, in East Hampshire. As a Knight of the Garter, he was given a state funeral in St. George's Chapel at Windsor Castle and buried in the local churchyard at Binstead, where a simple stone marks his grave. Tributes came from all over the world, from national leaders to wartime commanders to men who had served with Montgomery in the victorious Eighth Army. Perhaps the finest accolade came from Bradley, who put aside old enmities to send a wreath signed, "Dear Monty. Goodbye and thanks. Brad."[7]

EPILOGUE

The Soldier's Soldier

BEFORE HIS DEATH IN 1976, MONTGOMERY CLAIMED TO FRIENDS THAT "the rats will get at me," recognizing that his many enemies would attack him when he was no longer there to defend himself. It was not an inaccurate assessment. Many enemies and fair-weather friends had been upset by the publication of his *Memoirs*, and at the time of his passing, Montgomery's wartime reputation was already being reappraised, frequently in a pejorative way. In an assessment for *The Times* published the day after Montgomery's death, Sir Michael Howard, regius professor of history at Oxford and a wartime infantry officer, doubted if his subject could be counted as one of the great captains—or even "as one of the truly outstanding figures of the Second World War."[1] That set the tone for some vigorous revisionism, and as Montgomery had feared, the critics were not inclined to be kind. Three decades later, in his history of the D-Day operations, the historian Antony Beevor claimed that Montgomery had almost single-handedly destroyed the American alliance and that his attitude "constituted a diplomatic disaster of the first order."[2] He was also critical of Montgomery's handling of the fighting at Caen in June 1944, especially the aerial bombardment of the city. Somewhere beyond those two extreme views, Montgomery's reputation has to be subjected to a more objective analysis.

As has been noted, his behavior towards his American colleagues was frequently preposterous and intolerant, and it compares badly with the excellent cooperation that existed between British and U.S. commanders during the Korean War (1950–1953) and also in the coalition operations in Iraq and Afghanistan at the beginning of the twenty-first century. At the conclusion of the first phase of the fighting in Iraq in 2003, U.S. Secretary of Defense Donald Rumsfeld was moved to say that "America has no finer ally than the United Kingdom," and in that conflict the transatlantic military alliance was secure.[3] While Montgomery's attitudes do not wholly deserve Eisenhower's postwar assessment that he was a "psychopath," they do leave a question mark over his qualities as a commander of soldiers. He was guilty of recasting the facts to show his own actions and thinking in a good light, but that is not an uncommon failing among leaders. Both Bradley and Eisenhower did much the same in promoting their own contributions to the war effort in their memoirs. However, to deny Montgomery a place in the pantheon of the Second World War is a big step too far. Even the Germans respected him: Field Marshal Gerd von Rundstedt compared him to a racehorse that was expected to win and usually did, while General Erwin Rommel said that his opponent in North Africa never made a serious strategic mistake.

Montgomery might have been wrong-headed on occasion, and his overblown assertions of everything having gone according to plan were not always correct, but he remains one of the architects of the Allied victory, not only in North Africa but also in northwest Europe following the D-Day operations. Even in Normandy, his belief that Caen was the crucible of the battle was vindicated by events. By wearing down Rommel's panzer forces—albeit at great cost to the British and Canadian armies—considerable pressure was taken off General Omar Bradley's U.S. First Army at St. Lô. It is also fair to say that the actions at Caen helped to prevent the intervention of the German Fifteenth Army in Pas de Calais. Had Montgomery been a more diplomatic general or maintained open and regular contact with Eisenhower's headquarters, many of the misunderstandings might not have arisen.

In the greater scheme of things, Montgomery cannot be compared with such illustrious British predecessors as the Duke of Marlborough or the Duke of Wellington, but he is still the greatest British field commander of modern times, and his reputation has not been surpassed in more recent conflicts such as the Falklands (1982) or the Gulf War (1991). His reputation was not based merely on good publicity and headline grabbing—however much his personal enemies might have claimed that to be the case—rather, it was based on a mixture of military virtues that lie at the heart of any successful commander. Five in particular stand out to explain the success of this unusual, highly motivated, and, on occasion, damnably difficult soldier: training, planning, tactics, control, and morale.

First and foremost, throughout his career, Montgomery insisted on the primacy of sound training, and at all times he made sure that his soldiers understood what was expected of them so that they knew their tasks inside out. Without that solid basis, Montgomery reckoned that operations would end in failure, and he did not exempt higher-ranking officers. Central to the importance of sound training was a belief in high standards of physical and mental fitness, and this, too, applied to all ranks—senior officers unable to complete training runs were quickly dismissed or found other jobs.

Tough and realistic live-firing exercises also formed part of Montgomery's routine, the object being to prepare men as adequately as possible for the shock of battle. Most of the training regimes were devised by him, and woe betide anyone who paid them only lip service. At the same time, Montgomery was not keen on overly strict, formal battle-drill training, on the grounds that it stymied freedom of action by unit commanders and discouraged initiative. Never afraid to display ruthlessness toward inefficient or "useless" commanders who failed to meet his mark, Montgomery operated a strict and unyielding regime based on the maintenance of exceptionally high standards and a stringent adhesion to his orders. In that respect he was not dissimilar to General George S. Patton, a general with whom he had much in common as a trainer of soldiers and a willingness to do battle with his superior officers.

The emphasis on sound training sprung from the need to preserve lives and reduce casualties, a responsibility he felt that every good commander should accept. In that respect he would have approved of the professionalism lately shown by NATO commanders in Afghanistan, where steps have been taken to keep military and civilian casualties to a minimum. In today's counterinsurgency wars, it has become an article of faith that a commander will be cautious with soldiers' lives, especially against unyielding enemies such as the Taliban, who practice the exact opposite.

Montgomery has been criticized for being overcautious and refusing battle until he had built up a numerical superiority over the enemy. But from El Alamein onward, he revealed himself as a master of the *Materielschlacht*. This involved the inexorable buildup of superior manpower and supplies to levels that the opposition could not match. That helped to account for his desert victories at Alam Halfa and El Alamein. After the war, Montgomery's critics within the army argued that he owed his success to nothing more than this tactic of overwhelming force. To this argument Churchill responded: "I know why you all hate him. You are jealous: he is better than you are. Ask yourself these questions. What is a general for? Answer: to win battles. Did he win them without much slaughter? Yes. So what are you grumbling about?"[4]

But Montgomery's success was not simply a matter of math and weaponry. Before any engagement with the enemy, he would produce meticulous plans for the forthcoming battle so that all commanders and the forces under them knew their responsibilities. In addition to issuing comprehensive written orders, Montgomery also spent time briefing his commanders personally, and an important corollary to this process was a willingness to meet as many men as possible. On a purely operational level, on taking over command of the Eighth Army, he insisted on the importance of the division as the main fighting force and put a stop to the battle group system in which "divisions were split up into bits and pieces all over the desert."[5] Above all, Montgomery believed that operational training had to be geared toward the creation of the best military environment for a conscript army composed of civilian soldiers who would return to ordinary life once the war was over. It is a concept that has been adopted by today's all-volunteer armies, which operate in challenging conditions that are not always understood by the civilian population at home. For the British and U.S. armies, the present-day operations in Iraq and Afghanistan are cases in point.

❖

As a field commander Montgomery came into his own when he was directing a set-piece battle. While he was not a master tactician in the mold of Hannibal or Napoleon, Montgomery had a thorough understanding of what was needed to defeat whatever enemy was ranged against him. Not everything he did went according to plan, and he was frequently guilty of recasting unfavorable histories, but before any battle he took immense care in determining the tactics to be used. Luckily, he also had the gift of being able to communicate his tactical ideas to others using simple language and plain speech.

In no other wartime episode was this better demonstrated than when he assumed tactical control of the Allied forces in the run-up to the D-Day operations in the spring of 1944. Even Bradley, not always an admirer, later admitted that Montgomery came into his own when he produced the plans that got the Allied forces across the English Channel: "Monty's incomparable talent for the 'set' battle—the meticulously planned offensive—made him invaluable in the overlord assault. For the Channel crossing was patterned to a rigid plan; nothing was left to chance or improvisation in command. Until we gained the beachhead, we were to put our faith in The Plan."[6]

An essential ingredient in Montgomery's leadership in battle was the need to "get a grip" on what was happening and then to control the outcome. The phrase punctuated much of his thinking on the subject and he was contemptuous of anyone who failed to also grasp the situation. As a result, he not only had to possess a thorough understanding of his own plans, spending long hours preparing and then refining his judgment, he also had to make sure that his thinking trickled down to his divisional commanders. Hand in hand with his mastery of the battleplan were the supreme confidence and resolve he brought to the art of command. Although he may have appeared bumptious or opinionated, Montgomery's self-possession was infectious and inspired tremendous confidence in those under his command. Many of his staff officers later spoke with gratitude about the poise he exhibited in the tense moments before battle was engaged.

Throughout his greatest triumph at El Alamein, he continuously insisted to his junior commanders that he had no intention of abandoning the initiative by loosening his own control of the battle: "I won't react to Rommel. Rommel will react to me," he told many of them during the battle. In view of the outcome, it was a prescient comment.

✦

Like all great generals, Montgomery placed a premium on the maintenance of morale among the men in the armies under his command. During the First World War he had witnessed firsthand the deleterious effects of poor planning and ineffectual communications in dealing with citizen soldiers, and as a consequence he made the care of his men a lifelong pursuit. He insisted that they be provided with adequate equipment, and his attention to detail extended to little things such as ensuring that their mail got through to them. In earlier conflicts, as Montgomery had observed, scant regard was paid to the welfare of soldiers in the field, but under his direction, all that changed in the Second World War, and it is central to the way the British army (and all good armies) operates today. Greater attention is paid to the creature comforts of soldiers on operations; medical care has improved, so that wounded soldiers have a better chance of surviving; and there is (or should be) ample rest and recreation. Another of Montgomery's legacies was the requirement for modern commanders to be known to their men outside their headquarters. Soldiers in Montgomery's forces readily recognized the physical presence of the man who commanded them and were grateful for the many opportunities he took to speak to them. He had a gift for making them feel that they knew him personally and that he cared deeply about what would happen to them.

Thanks to these thoughtful gestures, Montgomery's soldiers knew that he would not ask them to do anything he was not prepared to do himself. It did not derive from a desire to cultivate popularity, but from his integral belief that soldiers needed to be inspired, as he set out to do when he took over the demoralized Eighth Army in August 1942. Encouraging men to believe that they can rise above themselves and master their doubts and fears is one of the marks of a great commander. Whatever his other faults, Monty was just that.

Notes

Introduction

1. Lieutenant-Colonel Trumbull Warren, "The Surrender of the German Armed Forces," in Nigel Hamilton, *Monty: The Field Marshal 1944–1976* (London: Hamish Hamilton, 1986), p. 502.
2. "Victory in Europe: Monty's Moment," *Time*, May 14, 1945.
3. Signal to CIGS, May 3, 1945. Hamilton, *Monty: The Field Marshal*, pp. 505–506.
4. Bernard Law Montgomery, *Memoirs* (London: William Collins, 1958), pp. 338–340.

Chapter One: An Uncertain Education

1. Maud Montgomery, *I Remember, I Remember* (Belfast: W. & G. Baird, 1945), p. 25.
2. Geoffrey Stephens, "Montgomery, Henry Hutchinson (1847–1932)," *Australian Dictionary of Biography* (Melbourne: Melbourne University Press, 1986), vol. 10, pp. 558–559.
3. Stephens, "H. H. Montgomery, The Mutton Bird Bishop," University of Tasmania Occasional Paper 39 (Hobart: University of Tasmania, 1985), p. 12.
4. Alan Moorehead, *Montgomery* (London: Hamish Hamilton, 1946), p. 20.
5. Bernard Law Montgomery, *Memoirs* (London, William Collins, 1958), p. 18.
6. Brian Montgomery, *A Field Marshal in the Family* (London: Constable, 1973), p. 111.
7. Montgomery, *Memoirs,* p. 17.
8. Maud Montgomery, *Bishop Montgomery* (London: Society for the Propagation of the Gospel, 1933), p. 52.

9. Montgomery, *Memoirs*, p. 21.
10. *The Pauline*, November 1906, quoted in Nigel Hamilton, *Monty: The Making of a General* (New York: McGraw-Hill, 1981), p. 44.
11. Montgomery, *Memoirs*, p. 29.
12. Letter to his mother, July 12, 1916. Hamilton, *Monty: The Making of a General*, pp. 107–108.
13. Letter to his mother, November 8, 1917. Hamilton, *Monty: The Making of a General*, p. 129.

Chapter Two: Peacetime Soldiering

1. *Owl Pie*, Christmas 1920, quoted in Nigel Hamilton, *Monty: The Making of a General* (New York: McGraw-Hill, 1981), p. 152.
2. Editorial, *Irish Times*, April 13, 1921.
3. Editorial, *An t-Oglach, The Official Organ of the Irish Volunteers*, October 21, 1921.
4. Montgomery to A. E. Percival, April 1922. Hamilton, *Monty: The Making of a General*, p. 160.
5. Hamilton, *Monty: The Making of a General*, p. 190.
6. Anonymous, *The Antelope, The Journal of the Royal Warwickshire Regiment*, January 1926.
7. Hamilton, *Monty: The Making of a General*, p. 226.
8. Ibid, p. 259.

Chapter Three: The Drift to War

1. Nigel Hamilton, *Monty: The Making of a General* (New York: McGraw-Hill, 1981), p. 280.
2. Hew Strachan, *The Politics of the British Army* (Oxford: Clarendon Press, 1997), pp. 153–157.
3. Hamilton, *Monty: The Making of a General*, p. 290.
4. *Palestine: Statement of Policy,* Cmd. 6019 (May 1939).
5. Robin McNish, *Iron Division: The History of the 3rd Division 1809–2000* (Headquarters 3rd UK Division, 2000), p. 71.
6. Alex Danchev and Daniel Todman, *War Diaries 1939–1945, Field Marshal Lord Alanbrooke* (London: Weidenfeld & Nicolson, 2001), p. 12 (hereafter *Alanbrooke War Diaries*).
7. United Kingdom, War Office, NA WO197/148 War Diary 2 Corps, G. Ops, National Archives, Kew.
8. Bernard Law Montgomery, *Memoirs* (London: William Collins, 1958), p. 61.
9. Ibid.

10. Bernard Law Montgomery, *The Path to Leadership* (London: William Collins, 1961), pp. 41–44.
11. Winston Churchill, speech in House of Commons, June 4, 1940.
12. *Alanbrooke War Diaries*, pp. 71–73.
13. Hamilton, *Monty: The Making of a General*, p. 393.

Chapter Four: Full of Binge

1. United Kingdom, War Office, "British Expeditionary Force, France: War Diaries, Second World War, 3rd Infantry Division," PRO WO 167, June 17, 1940, National Archives, Kew.
2. Bernard Law Montgomery, *Memoirs* (London: William Collins, 1958), p. 63.
3. Alexander Greenwood, *Auchinleck* (Durham, England: Pentland Press, 1990), pp. 104–105.
4. Ibid., pp. 109–110.
5. Brooke to Montgomery, August 5, 1940. Nigel Hamilton, *Monty: The Making of a General* (New York: McGraw-Hill, 1981), p. 433.
6. *Alanbrooke War Diaries*, pp. 289–296.
7. Ibid., p. 290.
8. Ibid., pp. 289–296.
9. Ibid, pp. 246–249.
10. Hamilton, *Monty: The Making of a General*, p. 478.
11. *8th Army Training Memorandum No.1: The Approach to Training*, PRO WO169/3926, August 10, 1942, National Archives, Kew.
12. Montgomery, *Memoirs*, pp. 91–96.

Chapter Five: Desert Victory: The Battles of Alam Halfa
and El Alamein

1. Bernard Law Montgomery, *Memoirs* (London: William Collins, 1958), pp. 622–624.
2. Francis de Guingand, *Operation Victory* (London: Hodder and Stoughton, 1947), pp. 136–137.
3. United Kingdom, War Office, 169/3937 *War Diary 8th Army HQ 'I' Section*, July–December, 1942, National Archives.
4. Paul Freyberg, *Bernard Freyberg VC: Soldier of Two Nations* (London: Hodder & Stoughton, 1991), p. 386.
5. Nigel Hamilton, *Monty: The Making of a General* (New York: McGraw-Hill, 1981), p. 744.
6. Ibid., p. 756.
7. Patrick Delaforce, *Monty's Highlanders: 51st Highland Division in World War Two* (Brighton, England: Tom Donovan, 1997), p. 33.

8. Hamilton, *Monty: The Making of a General*, pp. 761–774.

9. Field Marshal Lord Carver, *El Alamein* (London: Batsford, 1962), 116–117.

10. Hamilton, *Monty: The Making of a General*, pp. 789–797.

Chapter Six: Pursuit into Tunisia

1. *Alanbrooke War Diaries*, p. 378.

2. Ibid., p. 378.

3. Montgomery to Brooke, March 6, 1943. Nigel Hamilton, *Monty: Master of the Battlefield 1942–1944* (London: Hamish Hamilton, 1983), pp. 171–181.

4. United Kingdom, War Office, "Allied Forces, North Africa (British Element): War Diaries, Second World War , 51st (Highland) Division," PRO WO 175, March 22, 1943, National Archives.

5. Hamilton, *Monty: Master of the Battlefield*, p. 206.

6. Alexander to Montgomery, March 29, 1943. Hamilton, *Monty: Master of the Battlefield*, p. 210.

7. Montgomery to Alexander, April 4, 1943. Ibid., p. 211.

8. Harry C. Butcher, *My Three Years with Eisenhower* (New York: Simon & Schuster, 1946), p. 616.

9. Field Marshal Erwin Rommel, *The Rommel Papers*, ed. Basil Liddell Hart (London: William Collins, 1953) p. 523.

10. *Alanbrooke War Diaries*, p. 418.

Chapter Seven: Operation Husky

1. Martin Gilbert, *Churchill: A Life* (London: Heinemann, 1991), p 767.

2. Nigel Hamilton, *Monty: Master of the Battlefield 1942–1944* (London: Hamish Hamilton, 1983), p. 227.

3. Ibid., p. 262.

4. Carlo D'Este, *A Genius for War: A Life of George S. Patton* (New York: Harper Collins, 1995), p. 494.

5. *Alanbrooke War Diaries*, p. 407.

6. Hamilton, *Monty: Master of the Battlefield*, p. 295.

7. Ibid., pp. 302–303.

8. Montgomery diary in Hamilton, *Monty: Master of the Battlefield*, p. 320.

9. Montgomery to Alexander, July 25, 1943. Ibid., p. 320.

Chapter Eight: The Invasion of Europe

1. Nigel Hamilton, *Monty: Master of the Battlefield 1942–1944* (London: Hamish Hamilton, 1983), p. 413.

2. Ibid., pp. 426–431.
3. *Alanbrooke War Diaries*, pp. 496–497.
4. Max Hastings, *Overlord: D-Day and the Battle for Normandy 1944* (London: Michael Joseph, 1984), p. 31.
5. "Talk to Generals," January 13, 1944, in Hamilton, *Monty: Master of the Battlefield*, p. 493.
6. Omar N. Bradley, *A Soldier's Story* (New York: Henry Holt, 1951), pp. 239–242.
7. Hastings, *Overlord*, p. 32.
8. Antony Beevor, *D-Day: The Battle for Normandy* (London: Viking, 2009), pp. 72–73.

Chapter Nine: Normandy: From D-Day to Deadlock

1. Stephen Ambrose, *D-Day June 6 1944: The Climactic Battle of World War II* (New York: Simon & Schuster, 1994), p. 50.
2. John McGregor, *The Spirit of Angus: The War History of the County's Battalion of The Black Watch* (Chichester, England: Phillimore, 1988), p. 123.
3. Patrick Delaforce, *Monty's Highlanders: 51ˢᵗ Highland Division in World War Two* (Brighton, England: Tom Donovan, 1997), p. 138.
4. J. B. Salmond, *The History of the 51st Highland Division 1939–1945* (Edinburgh: William Blackwood, 1953), p. 145.
5. Delaforce, *Monty's Highlanders*, pp. 141–146.
6. Antony Beevor, *D-Day: The Battle for Normandy* (London: Viking, 2009), p. 323.
7. Harry C. Butcher, *My Three Years with Eisenhower* (New York: Simon & Schuster, 1946), p. 616.
8. Nigel Hamilton, *Monty: Master of the Battlefield 1942–1944* (London: Hamish Hamilton, 1983), p. 731.
9. L. F. Ellis, *Victory in the West* (London: HMSO, 1962), vol. I, pp. 344–345.
10. Air Marshal Sir Arthur Coningham, 2nd TAF Operations Report, PRO AIR 20/1593, National Archives, Kew.
11. Hamilton, *Monty: Master of the Battlefield*, pp. 717–726.
12. *Alanbrooke War Diaries*, p. 571.
13. Martin Blumenson (ed.), *The Patton Papers 1940–1945* (Boston: Houghton Mifflin, 1982), pp. 477–482.
14. Hamilton, *Monty: Master of the Battlefield*, pp. 758–759.
15. Omar N. Bradley, with Clay Blair, *A General's Life: The Autobiography of General of the Army Omar N. Bradley* (New York: Simon & Schuster, 1983), pp. 261–266.
16. Sir Basil Liddell Hart, *History of the Second World War* (London: Cassell, 1970), p. 568.

Chapter Ten: A Lost Port and a Bridge Too Far

1. "Notes on Future Operations" in Nigel Hamilton, *Monty: Master of the Battlefield 1942–1944* (London: Hamish Hamilton, 1983), pp. 816–817.
2. Lord Moran, *Churchill: The Struggle for Survival 1940–1965* (London: Constable, 1966), p. 658.
3. H. G. Nicholas, ed., *Washington Despatches 1941–1945* (London: Weidenfeld & Nicolson, 1981), p. 418.
4. E.W.I.P. (Edgar W. I. Palamountain), *Taurus Pursuant: A History of 11th Armoured Division* (Germany: 11th Armoured Division, 1945), p. 118.
5. Chester Wilmot, *Struggle for Europe* (London: Collins, 1952), p. 486.
6. Bernard Law Montgomery, *Memoirs* (London: William Collins, 1958), pp. 284–287.
7. Nigel Hamilton, *Monty: The Field Marshal 1944–1976* (London: Hamish Hamilton, 1986), pp. 48–55.
8. Eric Larrabee, *Commander-in-Chief: Franklin Delano Roosevelt, His Lieutenants and Their War* (New York: Harper & Row, 1987), p. 479.
9. Montgomery to Brooke, September 12, 1944. Hamilton, *Monty: The Field Marshal*, pp. 57–58.
10. Hamilton, *Monty: The Field Marshal*, p. 74.
11. L. F. Ellis, *Victory in the West* (London: HMSO, 1962), vol. II, p. 237.

Chapter Eleven: A Falling Out in the Ardennes

1. Max Hastings, *Armageddon: The Battle for Germany 1944–45* (London: Macmillan, 2004), p. 70.
2. Omar N. Bradley, with Clay Blair, *A General's Life: The Autobiography of General of the Army Omar N. Bradley* (New York: Simon & Schuster, 1983), pp. 363–364.
3. *Alanbrooke War Diaries*, p. 600.
4. Carlo D'Este, *Eisenhower: A Soldier's Life* (New York: Henry Holt, 2002), pp. 656–657.
5. Ibid.
6. Bradley, *A General's Life*, p. 343.
7. Montgomery to Brooke, November 17, 1944. Nigel Hamilton, *Monty: The Field Marshal 1944–1976* (London: Hamish Hamilton, 1986), pp. 139–140.
8. Bradley memorandum, December 13, 1944. Hamilton, *Monty: The Field Marshal*, p. 163.
9. Peter Elstob, *Hitler's Last Offensive* (London: Martin Secker & Warburg, 1971), pp. 67–77.
10. Hamilton, *Monty: The Field Marshal*, pp. 210–218.
11. Hastings, *Armageddon*, p. 254.

12. Elstob, *Hitler's Last Offensive*, p. 364.

13. Dwight D. Eisenhower, *Crusade in Europe* (Garden City, NY: Doubleday, 1950), p. 356.

Chapter Twelve: Crossing the Rhine

1. Chester Wilmot, *Struggle for Europe* (London: Collins, 1952) p. 668.

2. Lieutenant-Colonel R. H. Paterson, *Pontius Pilate's Bodyguard: A History of The First or Royal Regiment of Foot The Royal Scots (The Royal Regiment)*, vol. II 1919–2000 (Edinburgh: The Royal Scots History Committee, 2000), p. 239.

3. David Fraser, *And We Shall Shock Them: The British Army in the Second World War* (London: Hodder & Stoughton, 1983), p. 390.

4. Ian C. Cameron, *History of the Argyll and Sutherland Highlanders, 7th Battalion from El Alamein to Germany* (London: Thomas Nelson, 1946), p. 186.

5. Sir Martin Lindsay, *So Few Got Through* (London: William Collins, 1946), p. 223.

6. Cameron, *History of the Argyll and Sutherland Highlanders*, p. 186.

7. Wilfred Miles, *The Life of a Regiment* vol. V, *The Gordon Highlanders, 1919–1945* (Aberdeen: Aberdeen University Press, 1961), p. 346.

8. Nigel Hamilton, *Monty: The Field Marshal 1944–1976* (London: Hamish Hamilton, 1986), p. 420.

9. Lloyd Clark, *Arnhem: Jumping the Rhine 1944 and 1945, The Greatest Airborne Battle in History* (London: Headline Review, 2008), p. 335.

10. *Alanbrooke War Diaries*, p. 677.

11. Dwight D. Eisenhower, *Crusade in Europe* (Garden City, NY: Doubleday, 1950), p. 433.

12. Hamilton, *Monty: The Field Marshal*, p. 492.

13. Miles, *The Life of a Regiment*, p. 353.

14. Montgomery to Brooke, May 2, 1945. Hamilton, *Monty: The Field Marshal*, p. 499.

15. B. G. Horrocks, *A Full Life* (London: Collins, 1960), p. 240.

Chapter Thirteen: Cold War Warrior

1. David Fraser, *And We Shall Shock Them: The British Army in the Second World War* (London: Hodder & Stoughton, 1983), pp. 395–396.

2. Bill Jackson and Dwin Bramall, *The Chiefs: The Story of the United Kingdom Chiefs of Staff* (London: Brassey's, 1992), p. 268.

3. Ibid., p. 273.

4. Nigel Hamilton, *Monty: The Field Marshal 1944–1976* (London: Hamish Hamilton, 1986), pp. 656–659.
5. Ibid., pp.883–897.
6. Stephen Ambrose, *Eisenhower: Soldier, General of the Army, President-Elect 1890–1952*, (New York: Simon & Schuster, 1983), p. 264.
7. Hamilton, *Monty: The Field Marshal,* p. 947.

Epilogue: The Soldier's Soldier

1. Sir Michael Howard, "How will History judge Lord Montgomery's Generalship?", *The Times*, March 25, 1976.
2. Antony Beevor, *D-Day: The Battle for Normandy* (London: Viking, 2009), pp. 522–523.
3. Trevor Royle, "America Has No Finer Ally Than the United Kingdom," *Veterans of Foreign Wars*, September 2003, pp. 34–38.
4. Beevor, *D-Day*, pp. 522–523.
5. Nigel Hamilton, *Monty: The Making of a General* (New York: McGraw-Hill, 1981), p. 630.
6. Omar N. Bradley, with Clay Blair, *A General's Life: The Autobiography of General of the Army Omar N. Bradley* (New York: Simon & Schuster, 1983), pp. 239–242.

Index

Maginot Line, 45
maneuver warfare, 78
Manteuffel, Hasso von,
  147, 149
Mareth Line, 81–4
Marshall, George, 59, 86, 89,
  93, 105–6, 163–4, 172–3
*Mechanised and Armoured
  Formations* (1929), 24
mechanized warfare, 24, 51–2
Memoirs (1958), 177–8, 179
Mesopotamian campaign
  (1915–1918), 52
Messe, Giovanni, 81
Messina, battle of (1943),
  94–100
Messines, battle of (1917), 16
military appointments
  (Montgomery)
  battalion command, 30–1
  brevet-major, 19
  brigade major, 16, 27
  British task force command, 58
  Chief of Imperial General
    Staff, 170–4
  chief instructor at Indian
    Staff College, 33
  chief staff officer (GSO1), 18
  divisional chief of staff, 27
  Eighth Army command, 63–9
  Eighth Infantry Division
    command, 39
  General Staff Officer,
    Second Grade, 16, 22, 27
  NATO Deputy Supreme
    Allied Commander,
    Europe, x, 175–6
  Ninth Infantry Brigade
    command, 35–6
  senior officer in Palestine, 32
  17th Royal Fusiliers
    command, 22
  South-Eastern Command, 61
  and Staff College, 22–4,
    28–9
  staff officer, 16, 18, 22, 28
  Third Infantry Division
    command, 41–2
  21st Army Group
    command, 1–3
military character,
  (Montgomery), 1, 3–5, 24,
  32–3, 128, 135, 139–41,

146, 169–72, 177–8,
  179–81
military rank (Montgomery)
  brevet lieutenant-colonel, 28
  captain, 17
  colonel, 33
  field marshal, vii, 1, 22,
    73–4, 129
  general, viii, 77
  knighted, 77
  lieutenant-colonel, 18
  lieutenant-general, 53
  major, 16, 19, 27
  major-general, 39
  reduction in, viii, 19
military strategy
  (Montgomery), 41, 183–5
  See "binge"; "directed
    telescope"; "gallopers";
    "grip"
military training
  (Montgomery), x, 15–18,
  26–32, 38–9, 44–5,
  53–5, 60–1, 78, 181–2
  See "grip"
Model, Walter, 131
modern warfare, 18, 29–30
Montgomery, Bernard Law
  abstemiousness, 14–15,
    79, 176
  ancestry of, 7
  athleticism of, 12–13, 181
  birth of, 7
  childhood, vii, 7–11
  comparisons with Rommel,
    77–9
  death of, 178, 179
  death of wife, 36–7
  divisiveness of, *See* military
    character
  education, *See* Royal Military
    College at Sandhurst; St.
    Paul's School
  funeral of, 178
  and German surrender
    (WWII), 1–3
  health of, viii, 16, 42, 69–70
  marriage, 28–9, 36
  "Monty" (nickname), vii, 169
  post-World War I, 21–2
  public life of, 177–8
  retirement from military
    (1958), 176

teenage years, 11–13
  trademark look of, 79
  and violent incident (as
    youth), 13
  wounding of, viii, 16
  writing of, 16–17, 26, 39,
    41, 47, 177–8
  Viscount of Alamein, 73–4,
    170
  See leadership; military
    appointments; military
    character; military rank;
    military training
Montgomery, Betty Hobart
  Carver (wife), 29, 36–7
Montgomery, David (son),
  29, 36
Montgomery, Henry
  Hutchinson (father), 7–9,
  11–12
Montgomery, Hugh (cousin),
  25
Montgomery, Maud Farrar
  (mother), 7–12
Montgomery, Robert
  (grandfather), 8
"Monty moonlight," 127–8
Morgan, Frederick, 107–9
Mussolini, Benito, 38, 41, 99

Napoleon I of France, 167, 183
Napoleon III of France, 50
National Government, 37
Nazi Germany, 38, 42, 77, 89,
  164–5
Near East Command, 57
New Zealand divisions, 66–9,
  73, 75, 82–4
IX Corps (British), 16–17, 26
XIX Corps (French), 80–1
Ninth Army (U.S.), 145, 155,
  157–8, 160, 162–3, 166
9th Armoured Brigade
  (British), 73
9th Infantry Brigade (British),
  33, 35–6
Ninth Panzer Division
  (German), 137
Normandy, invasion of
  (1944), ix, 4, 93, 105,
  114, 117–28, 130–1,
  143, 148, 178, 179–81,
  183–4